MORE ADVANCE PRAISE FOR *STRONG KIDS, HEALTHY KIDS*

"In nearly 30 years as a medical reporter, the one thing that I continue to be amazed at is how much of what we once "knew" in health and medicine has proven to be wrong. From stem cells in adult hearts and brains to the causes and treatment of disease, medical knowledge is ever changing and growing. To that list we can now add the myth that weight training is dangerous for kids. Fred Hahn not only dispels the misconception that it's harmful, he's shown that it's beneficial in numerous ways, not the least of which may be weight control for our increasingly sedentary young people. Better yet, Fred has shown us how to strength-train our children in a safe, effective, and, yes, even enjoyable manner. This is a book all parents need...for the health of their children."

    —**Dr. Max Gomez,** Medical Correspondent for CBS-TV, New York

"Are you concerned that your kid is weak, obese, even headed toward Type 2 diabetes? If so, you will find the answers on how to help your kid become strong, healthy, and fit in Fred Hahn's new book, *Strong Kids, Healthy Kids.* And the treatment is not some dangerous drug. Rather it is whole foods, pure water, exercise, and strength training à la Fred Hahn."

    —**Dr. Bruce West,** Founder, HealthAlert.com

Strong Kids, Healthy Kids

The Revolutionary Program for Increasing Your
Child's Fitness in 30 Minutes a Week

FREDRICK HAHN

Foreword by Wayne L. Westcott, Ph.D.

AMERICAN MANAGEMENT ASSOCIATION

New York • Atlanta • Brussels • Chicago • Mexico City • San Francisco
Shanghai • Tokyo • Toronto • Washington, D. C.

Special discounts on bulk quantities of AMACOM books are available to corporations, professional associations, and other organizations. For details, contact Special Sales Department, AMACOM, a division of American Management Association, 1601 Broadway, New York, NY 10019.

Tel.: 212-903-8316. Fax: 212-903-8083.
Web site: www.amacombooks.org

This publication is designed to provide accurate and authoritative information in regard to the subject matter covered. It is sold with the understanding that the publisher is not engaged in rendering legal, accounting, or other professional service. If legal advice or other expert assistance is required, the services of a competent professional person should be sought.

Library of Congress Cataloging-in-Publication Data

Hahn, Fredrick.
    Strong kids, healthy kids : the revolutionary program for increasing your child's fitness in 30 minutes a week / Fredrick Hahn.
        p. cm.
    Includes bibliographical references and index.
    ISBN-13: 978-0-8144-0942-8
    ISBN-10: 0-8144-0942-3

    1. Physical education for children.   2. Physical fitness for children. 3. Exercise for children. I. Title.

    GV443.H15 2008

    613.7'042–dc   222008027227

Printing Number

10 9 8 7 6 5 4 3 2 1

This book is dedicated to my daughters
GEORGIA and **AMBER**
and to all the children of the earth.

Contents

Acknowledgments

All books are collaborative works and as such are labors of friendships. Among the many friends who have made this book possible, Robin Dellabough gets a huge thanks as her keen eye and writing skills kept me on track and clear.

To Jacquie Flynn, executive editor, and the entire staff at AMACOM, you all are the best.

To my agent, Lisa DiMona, who made it possible for this book to become a book and for her bright and positive attitude.

To Eugene Thong, Tommy Day, Neil Holland, Irene Elias, and Teri Evans, who along with me instruct the kids at Serious Strength—the best team of instructors you could ever have. Also Tanya Trombly and Hannah Neighbor, Serious Strength's management team, who keep Serious Strength running like a well-oiled machine.

To Wayne Westcott, Ph.D., who provided me with (and conducted) much of the research and information for the book.

To the parents of the children who train at Serious Strength. Good for you for such a commitment to your family!

Lastly, to my wife, Linda, who has helped me every step of the way and in every way and who keeps our kids healthy, happy, and strong. Love ya!

Foreword

Years ago there was a very popular monthly magazine titled *Strength and Health.* At first, I thought the words should be reversed, as health seemed to be a much broader and important life attribute than strength. However, after conducting research in the area of muscular fitness over the past 30 years, I now realize that for most practical purposes as your strength goes...so goes your health. Fred Hahn's new book, *Strong Kids, Healthy Kids,* is therefore a perfect title for showing the direction we need to take to enhance the health and fitness of our nation's young people.

As Fred clearly explains in his well-written text, the best time to be strong is during youth and the best time to develop strength is during youth. It's a perfect match, and yet one that is poorly understood by most people and rarely recommended by fitness or medical professionals. Part of the problem is the myth that, from an injury perspective, resistance exercise is unsafe and interferes with normal bone growth. Actually, nothing could be further from the truth. In all of the studies conducted on youth strength training over the past 30 years, not one has reported a serious injury resulting from supervised resistance exercise. With respect to bone, research reveals that preadolescent girls who strength train experience four times greater increase in bone mineral density during their ninth year of life than those who don't perform resistance exercise. Let it be clearly understood that the best time to develop a strong musculoskeletal system (for life) is during youth, and that the best way to achieve this is through a sensible strength training program.

Although some people may think that resistance exercise is boring, we have never had that response from our youth strength training program participants. Throughout 20 years of conducting youth strength training studies, our classes have averaged better than a 90 percent attendance rate and a 95 percent completion rate. Youth enjoy both the process and the product of sensible strength training, especially those children who are overweight. Whereas heavier children typically perform poorly in sports that involve speed, endurance, and agility, they generally use higher resistance than their lighter peers, which makes strength training a highly reinforcing physical activity for them.

As youth develop a stronger musculoskeletal system, they experience improved physical capacity and performance power, which encourages them to be more active and athletically inclined. Of course, more physical activity results in greater energy expenditure which leads to less body fat. First, resistance exercise is a vigorous activity that burns six to eight calories per minute when performed in a circuit-training format. Second, after a few weeks of regular resistance exercise, the new and conditioned muscle requires more energy for tissue remodeling and maintenance purposes 24 hours a day, resulting in a higher resting metabolism. As Fred explains clearly in his text, these advantageous aspects of strength training are major factors for calorie use and fat loss.

While strength training may be the most important physical activity for youth, it should be performed in a safe and effective manner. Fred wisely advises against fast and momentum-assisted strength training, as explosive movements with added resistance can place excessive stress on joint structures. Our research supports Fred's slow-speed exercise protocol for maximizing strength development and minimizing injury risk. Equally important, the recommended strength training programs can be successfully performed in a time-efficient manner.

Indeed, if there is one activity that boys and girls in our sedentary society should be doing for strength and health it is sensible strength training. *Strong Kids, Healthy Kids,* by fitness expert Fred Hahn, presents essential information and excellent guidelines for safely, effectively, and efficiently achieving these most desirable goals.

—Wayne L. Westcott, Ph.D.
Fitness Research Director,
South Shore YMCA

Introduction

"For the children will inherit our earth."
—FREDRICK HAHN

Have you ever said (or thought) any of these things about your kid:

- She needs to be in better shape.

- How come he seems to be out of breath during a game even though he's at practice five days a week?

- He's got to get stronger if he wants to make the team.

- They spend too much time watching TV, texting, and playing video games.

- How come he's so involved in sports, and is still too fat?

- She's skinny, but if she had to run anywhere, I think she'd keel over.

- I think what I'm feeding him is right, but how come he's still so heavy?

What are you doing about it? Perhaps you've read all the articles, watched all the specials, spoken to all the coaches, and now you have a plan—or, at least, you think you do. If your child is overfat* you know you should send your child to soccer camp, make him or her try out for the basketball team, throw out the television, insist on long family walks, and banish all fatty foods from the home.

If your child is weak and skinny, your plan is to do almost the same thing. If your kid's athletic, you do everything the coaches tell you and encourage your kid to follow the coach's advice. Do all this, and your son or daughter will slim down, beef up, improve athletic performance, and live happily, healthily ever after, correct?

Let me say right here and now that I will tell you—sometimes bluntly— that many widespread beliefs about fat loss, athletic performance, diet (a nasty little four-letter word), and exercise for kids are completely false, dangerous, and inane. I've got two daughters of my own whom I love as you love yours and I've had it up to here with the lies and misinformation.

Truth be told, almost all the so-called fitness programs for getting kids lean and strong are either wrong or misguided. Almost all the books on the subject of how kids should eat are wrong. As we all know, kids today are more unfit than ever before in history. Fewer kids walk or ride their bikes to school, work on farms, or carry heavy books. Mass transportation, minivans, and electric scooters have decreased the amount of

---

*I use the term *overfat* instead of overweight throughout the book because a child's weight isn't the real issue. Having too much fat is the issue. And by using this choice of words, we keep our eye on the target. Remember, there is nothing wrong with body fat. A certain amount is healthy and vital to health. But too much can be unhealthy. What your child weighs doesn't really matter; however, his body composition does matter. A large-boned, tall child may weigh in as overweight for his age, but he may be perfectly healthy and possess a normal and healthy level of body fat.

locomotion kids do: farming is now almost entirely motorized and electronic; heavy traffic makes riding a bike to school too dangerous in many places; and heavy textbooks are often replaced by their electronic counterparts. This is not, however, the main reason so many children today are overfat and unhealthy. Well, what should we do about it? What *can* we do about it?

All right, I'm going to tell you something shocking. Get ready. There is one type of exercise program that will not only solve all of these problems but also address, solve, and fix all of the previously mentioned queries and questions that parents, teachers, doctors, and other adults have. That exercise program is *weight training,* which is also known as strength training or resistance training.

WHAT ARE THE BENEFITS OF STRENGTH TRAINING FOR KIDS?

The benefits of strength training are profound and comprehensive, and include the following:

- Increased lean body mass (bone and muscle)

- Improved flexibility

- Improved body composition (less fat/more muscle)

- Improved base metabolic rate (calories burned)

- Increased muscle strength and power

- Decreased fat mass

- Gaining of confidence and self-esteem

- Improved general fitness

- Greater resistance to injury

- Reduction in the severity of injuries sustained during other physical activities

- Improvement in all aspects of cardiovascular health (cholesterol, blood pressure, aerobic endurance, power, and strength)

- Improved coordination

- Help in stabilizing blood sugar to offset type II diabetes

- Improvement in the ability to perform physical activities

- Encouragement of kids to participate in physical activities

Why do you need this book? Well, if the previous questions are ones that you've thought about, this book is your short, simple, and safe answer to improving your child's life in ways that no other type of exercise or eating plan can achieve. If you follow the program within this book, your kid will be given the best chance possible to run faster, jump higher, trim down, and gain confidence in ways that no other type of program offers. All the information is grounded in science. The plan is universal, meaning, all kids can benefit. The results, as you will see in Chapter 2, are profound and heartwarming. And the bonus is that it can work for you, too!

Strength Training for Kids

In this book, we are talking about a strength training program designed for kids. And the best part? It takes only 30 minutes of training a week.

This "miracle" cure is actually simple. In strength training, specifically, slow and controlled speed strength training, you do each exercise very slowly using an appropriate weight or resistance until the muscles being worked are totally fatigued or exhausted after several repetitions, generally lasting for

60 to 90 seconds per exercise. Why slow? Instead of letting momentum take over for a portion of the exercise (as happens when you jerk or toss a weight too fast), you push or resist the weight under control, asking the muscles alone to do all the work, which reaps a proportionately greater reward. And theoretically it's safer.

IS SLOW SPEED STRENGTH TRAINING SAFE FOR KIDS?

The American writer Mark Twain is known for his witty and poignant remarks. He is credited with having said: "The truth is easy to kill. But a lie well told is immortal."

I want to state up front and center that if done correctly and with proper supervision, weight lifting or strength training is completely safe for kids. I'm sure that you've heard around the playground and in the schoolyard that weight lifting is dangerous for children. Even some doctors still hold this myth as a truth. The common thought by people who don't know better is a fear of damage to the bone growth plates. Yet there has never been a single such case ever reported in medical literature. Others say it can delay a child's musculoskeletal development, when the opposite is true. Studies have proven that strength training actually benefits musculoskeletal growth in kids—dramatically so. In an eight-week study on fifth graders, 20 boys and girls strength trained twice a week for 20 minutes and improved their body composition almost twice as much as their nontrained peers[1]. In a similar study using 11th grade ice skaters, almost the exact same results were achieved.[2] In another study conducted over one year with nine-year-old girls, the results of strength training showed a 6 percent greater increase in bone density than those girls who did not strength train.[3] And while in this study a so-called high-impact strength training protocol was used, no injuries were reported. It is also important to note that the researchers in this study, after scrutinizing the data, determined that increases in muscle (lean) mass was the primary reason why bone density and all of the other positive outcomes were achieved.

DOES STRENGTH TRAINING DAMAGE GROWTH PLATES?

As mentioned earlier, one safety concern regarding weight lifting or strength training in children involves growth plates. The growth plate, also known as the *epiphyseal plate,* is the growing tissue near the end of the long bones in pre-adults. Every long bone has two or more growth plates at each end. The growth plate determines the ultimate length and shape of the adult bone. When growth is completed, which occurs at some point during adolescence, the growth plates close and are replaced by solid bone.

A common misconception is that strength training can somehow injure a child's growth plates. When and how this myth got started is a mystery. It is simply not true. Perhaps the myth was conjured up by the misconception of what strength training is. According to an article by the National Institutes of Health (NIH), the cause of most growth plate injuries is acute trauma such as a bad fall (gymnastics), a strong blow to a limb (football), or overuse (long-distance runners).

If you look at how most people lift weights, you see a violent and high-impact scene. It could be that experts or doctors knowing that growth plate injuries are caused by violent acts warned people off weight lifting for kids assuming that they could get hurt doing so. (Not bad advice if you ask me.) But weight lifting doesn't have to be such a violent affair.

FITNESS TRUE OR FALSE?
What Are the Fitness and Nutrition Myths and Misconceptions?

Do you know which of the following statements is true or false?

- It is unsafe for children to lift weights   T   F

- Inactivity is a cause of obesity in children   T   F

- Weight lifting makes muscles tight and inflexible   T   F

- Lifting weights makes you slow   T   F

- You don't need to lift weights if you're very active   T   F

- You need aerobic exercise everyday   T   F

- If you lift weights you still need aerobics   T   F

- Aerobics burn significant calories   T   F

- You need to stretch before and after you work out   T   F

- You need to warm up before you lift weights   T   F

- Aerobics makes your heart healthier   T   F

- Aerobics makes your lungs stronger   T   F

- Large muscles are tight and inflexible   T   F

- Heavy weights build bulky muscles   T   F

- Light weights build toned muscles   T   F

- Balance training improves balance   T   F

- Agility drills build agility   T   F

- Fitness testing accurately measures fitness   T   F

- Training fast with weights makes you fast on the field   T   F

Surprise! Every single one of the statements above is FALSE!

One of the foremost experts on exercise in this country, Wayne Westcott, Ph.D., has been involved in much of the research on the subject of children and strength training. In numerous articles and interviews, Westcott contends that there is not a shred of evidence to support the idea that strength training can injure a child's growth plates. In doing research for this book, I sure couldn't find any—and believe me, I looked!

In fact, with proper supervision, strength training is so safe for youngsters that there is no specific age limitation. Let me repeat, any child of any age can safely participate in a supervised strength training program. Having said that, not all young children can or will take instruction or follow directions well enough to perform the exercises safely or in a manner that will benefit them. As a parent, you have to determine for yourself if you think your child is mentally ready and capable of following the specific instructions for doing the exercises properly. In my training programs, I have seen children as young as six years old who are able to follow instructions properly in order to safely perform strength training exercises and benefit from them greatly. My own daughter Georgia was one of them.

However, my daughter Amber at the same age was (and still is) such a goofball that she would not take my instructions seriously. Now, even at age 7, she still has trouble concentrating on the specifics, and can maybe get through two exercises. After this, she just giggles, squirms, and starts making funny faces. Every kid is different. You don't want to make strength training a "have to." Ideally, you want to make it a "want to," and that can only happen when your child is mentally mature enough to take the instructions seriously. It surely doesn't hurt to try it out on your child to see if she's ready to give it a whirl. Remember, it is not dangerous in the least, and you might be surprised how they take to it.

IS STRENGTH TRAINING REALLY EFFECTIVE IN KIDS?

Absolutely! In one study, a group of ten-year-olds increased their overall strength by 74 percent, including a 41 percent increase in chest press strength, after only two months of strength training done twice a week.[4] They also increased their lean mass by two and a half pounds and significantly increased bone mineral density. Not only that but these gains were long lasting rather than short lived. Many other studies have shown similar effects. Even the Mayo Clinic endorses and supports properly supervised strength training for children.

According to Dr. Wescott, "In one of our public school studies, the underfit and overfat fifth graders who participated in a basic and brief strength training program gained significantly more muscle and lost twice as much fat as a matched group of students who did not perform a strength exercise. Perhaps, most important, the strength-trained students made such noticeable physical improvements that the strength exercises were subsequently included in the standard physical education program." This book will allow you to implement the same type of strength program that the kids in the aforementioned study performed, making your child faster, leaner, stronger, happier, and healthier.

To quote Avery Faigenbaum, Ph.D., a top researcher in the field of adolescent strength training:

> The potential benefits of youth strength training extend beyond an increase in muscular strength and may include favorable changes in selected health- and fitness-related measures. If appropriate training guidelines are followed, regular participation in a youth strength-training program has the potential to increase bone mineral density, improve motor performance skills, enhance sports performance, and better prepare our young athletes for the demands of practice and competition. Despite earlier concerns regarding the safety and efficacy of youth strength training, current public health

objectives now aim to increase the number of boys and girls age 6 and older who regularly participate in physical activities that enhance and maintain muscular fitness.[5]

The American Academy of Pediatrics, the American College of Sports Medicine, the National Institutes of Health, and the American Orthopedic Society for Sports Medicine are among the organizations providing a growing body of scientific evidence that proves strength training is a safe and effective method of conditioning for children. As you can see thus far, my overall approach to helping children become healthy and fit has a solid scientific basis. I have incorporated this scientific foundation in creating the most effective program possible for kids.

If every family followed my exercise and eating plan, childhood obesity in this country would greatly diminish and virtually vanish. Childhood Type 2 diabetes (caused by poor diet) would be eliminated. Young athletes would suffer fewer injuries on the playing field and sports performance would improve. Health-care costs would plummet because health problems associated with obesity and from sporting injuries would decrease markedly. You would no longer have to force your kids into sports or activities that they dread. And as a loving parent, you would beam with joy at the sight of your thriving, bright, powerful, healthy, confident, and energetic child. I guarantee it.

By and large, kids have an intuitive feel for their bodies. The experience of increased strength will give your child the confidence to do what he or she couldn't do before. For those kids who are not so in tune, strength training will help them become so. Instead of walking away from the monkey bars, they'll be going hand over hand like a lemur (or, at least, much better than they did previously) before you know it.

And as mentioned earlier, for the athletic child, the stronger she is, the better she will perform. Athletes at all ability levels, no matter what sport or physical activity they engage in, will improve.

SUCCESS STORIES

Ephraim B.

Ephraim is a slight-of-frame kid who enjoys art, video games, and sports. As bodies go, Ephraim is not what you would call robust. On top of this frailty, he suffers from many allergies and requires an inhaler for respiratory issues.

Ephraim's mom and dad have been clients of mine for many years. As Ephraim grew, they were interested in my youth strength training program and wondered if it would be beneficial for their son. "Yes!" I calmly said and explained the way it worked.

Ephraim began training and very shortly thereafter, his mom came in and said to me that his tennis coach was wondering what in the heck she was feeding him! Barely able to hit the ball over the net with authority, he was now absolutely crushing the ball.

Katya and Marc B.

The same thing happened to Katya, but not in tennis. Katya is an 11-year-old figure skater who after training with us for a little less than six months astounded her coach at how much higher her jumps were and the authority with which she stuck her landings. Katya's coach also remarked on the improvement in Katya's flexibility. Her brother Marc also experienced similar improvements in ice hockey. Marc's power skating, speed, and maneuvering improved dramatically.

Michael H.

When I first met Michael, he was a very active 12-year-old athlete. He got plenty of regular physical exercise in gym class. He also played basketball, soccer, and pick-up games with his family. Just what the doctor ordered, isn't it? Nevertheless,

Michael was overfat. In fact, according to standard health measures, Michael was obese. At 5 feet 3 inches, he weighed 146 pounds—the weight of a full-grown, lean man who is 5 feet 9 inches.

Michael is not alone. Not by a long shot. He is one of more than 9 million (and counting) overweight children in this country. The health risks associated with being overweight are well documented. They include abnormally high cholesterol, high blood pressure, Type 2 diabetes, and arthritis, as well as poor self-image and depression. Although the psychological toll is hard to measure, it is obvious that being self-conscious, teased, or unable to participate in certain activities does not make for a happy child.

Michael is one of the lucky ones. He began to strength train with me for two 15-minute sessions per week. Eight months later, Michael has grown two inches taller and at 5 feet 5 inches, he weighs just 113 pounds. He's become the strong man and a leading scorer on his basketball team. Not only has he lost 33 pounds (while continuing to grow), he has altered his body composition (ratio of fat to muscle), and become the happy, healthy, and strong child he was meant to be.

• • •

Strength training is the *only* proven form of exercise that alters body composition in children, and slow speed strength training is both safer and more effective than conventional strength training.

In my more than 20 years as a professional exercise trainer working with adults, I have witnessed the benefits of slow speed strength training. Numerous studies and ongoing scientific research have borne out my results. *Strong Kids, Healthy Kids* adapts safe, proven, and increasingly popular slow speed strength training to help children improve fitness, increase sports performance, and be healthy. With the simple program outlined in this book, any parent can help a child be his or her strongest, fittest self.

There is a lot of advice about fitness and nutrition that is misleading, if not downright wrong. It's time to break down these myths once and for all so that our kids can be healthy, fit, and strong. This book aims to change that misinformation, beginning with explaining the following practical truths that can actually help your child:

- *The more muscle mass, the greater the amount of calories burned at rest or during activity.* It's not a tremendous amount, but it is significant. A lot of experts correctly state that a pound of muscle only uses a handful of calories. They conclude from this fact that building muscle does not contribute much to an enhanced metabolic (calorie burning) rate. But what they gloss over is it is not just the *added* muscle tissue that contributes to a supercharged metabolism, it is the totality of the muscles being trained that counts as well. In other words, trained muscles use more calories than untrained muscles. So the more muscle you have, the higher your metabolism will be—at rest or when active. Therefore, the net metabolic effect of strength training on calories used at rest is much greater than just the additional muscle you gain. Nifty, eh? One study performed by researchers at Tufts University boosted the subject's metabolism by 6.8 percent after only 12 weeks of strength training.[6] Another study by researchers at the University of Maryland showed that after 16 weeks of strength training, the subject's metabolism zoomed by 7.7 percent.[7] So, if an 80-pound child was to increase her metabolism by 7 percent (to average it out), it would increase her caloric expenditure by nearly 100 calories per day—*doing nothing!* This may not seem like a lot, but it adds up. One hundred calories multiplied by 365 days a year equals 36,500 extra calories the child will burn in a year doing nothing, which tallies to 10 pounds! This helps to offset the additional calories kids often take in when Mom and Dad aren't looking.

  And consider what happens when the opposite occurs: A diet/exercise program that results in a loss of muscle tissue also lowers a child's metabolism. This can lead to weaker bones and muscles and decreased stability in joints and connective tissue. Research reveals that typical dieting regimens without strength training exercises *always* result in a loss of muscle tissue. Even strenuous aerobic activity while dieting does not completely prevent muscle loss.

- *Physical inactivity is not the cause of obesity.* Plenty of healthy-weight kids sit on their duffs and play with a Gameboy. The get-outside-and-get-some-fresh-air-and-exercise mantra parents have been screaming at their overfat kids is not the way to cure childhood obesity. Look at any middle-school playground and you will see active—yet still overfat—kids and teens. This is not to say that playing with a Gameboy is better than baseball. On the contrary, physical activity is vital to a child's healthy development. But it is not the cure for obesity.

- *Eating a low-fat diet is not the best way to lose body fat.* Neither is counting calories. (Note: I will give a parent on my Slow Burn regimen guidelines for how to lower their child's caloric intake only if it is excessively high.) The very best way to lose body fat and to stay lean is to eat the right types of calories. If you do, you don't have to worry about counting silly old calories. The fact is that there is no such thing as a fattening food—only fattening eating habits. I increase the amount of healthy fats and proteins in the child's diet and significantly reduce the amount of carbohydrates, especially refined carbohydrates (breads, pastas, bagels, etc.). I advise they eat more good fats (like avocados, olive oil, egg yolks, and so on), more fish, eggs, and meat, and ideally no grain products of any kind. That's right—no grain at all. Since fruits and veggies contain more fiber than grain products by a long shot, there's no need to worry about dietary fiber. I advise a plentiful amount of vegetables and some fruit for vitamins and minerals as well as for keeping the blood pH levels (and a host of other things) healthy. It is virtually impossible to become obese and unhealthy eating according to these guidelines.

As I've said, kids are not overfat because they are lazy, inactive, and eat too much fat. They are overfat because they eat too much, especially too many carbohydrates (sugar). This will be explained in detail in Chapter 3.

> **?** *DID YOU KNOW?* The more muscle you have, the speedier your metabolism?

ISN'T AEROBIC EXERCISE MORE IMPORTANT FOR MY CHILD'S HEALTH?

No. And there is a difference between aerobic exercise and cardiovascular exercise. All aerobic activities such as running or swimming require cardiovascular (heart and lung) work. But so do the power sports like strength training, wrestling, or sprinting. Strength training, performed properly, challenges the cardiovascular system more than adequately enough to keep your child's cardiovascular system healthy. Strength training alone will not make a child a champion runner or swimmer. For that you must attain a high level of skill at the sport. But she does not need to be an aerobic champion to have a healthy, strong cardiovascular system. If she already enjoys aerobic activities, adding slow speed strength training to her aerobic activities will allow her to perform these activities better, safer, and for many years to come because the muscles are really the engines of the body. The muscles are the boss of the body. The heart and lungs merely go along for the ride the muscles take them on. Moreover, slow speed strength training is all she needs to pass a routine physical exam with flying colors. Strength training is more potent than aerobics for all the benefits that a doctor checks in a routine physical exam, including cholesterol, blood pressure, body fat, insulin sensitivity, bone density, and more.

IS SLOWER BETTER?

First, let me quote from a well-respected exercise physiology publication: "At slow speeds the maximum number of cross-bridges can be formed. The more rapidly the actin and myosin filaments slide past one another,   the smaller the number of links that can be formed between the filaments in a unit of time and the less the amount of force is developed."[8] Boiled down, what this means is that if you move your limbs very quickly when lifting weights, the stimulus is less effective. Therefore, the quality of the contraction of the muscle is enhanced when the speed of movement of the muscle fibers is slow and when the speed is fast, the quality is decreased. We should always look to increase the quality of anything we do, so why should the work of the muscle be any different?

Research performed by Wayne Westcott, Ph.D., confirms this: "The study assessed a way to increase the intensity and effectiveness of resistance training by comparing training with a slower repetition speed to training with a conventional repetition speed. Slower repetition speed may effectively increase intensity throughout the lifting phase while decreasing momentum."[9]

What slow speed strength training does is improve the quality of the weight lifting program. And in my experience, it's the quality not the *quantity* of an exercise program that leads to superior results.

ABOUT THE BOOK

Strong Kids, Healthy Kids is for parents and kids. Chapter 1: The Slow Speed Training Program Basics is an overview of slow speed strength training, including its foundation, explanation of the program, and description of proper technique. Most important, it contains a guide for how you can become your child's personal trainer, gently and expertly encouraging kids to exercise the correct way with the correct weight and at the correct speed.

Chapter 2: The Slow Speed Exercises goes into detail about the specific exercises that kids will do for each session. You will need to coach younger children thoroughly as kids won't actually read the book. For older kids, the book is a good reference, but you should still keep an eye on most exercise sessions. I include ways to continue to encourage your child throughout the program, exercise by exercise, as well as including phrases and comments from my own training practice so that you can say the right thing at the right time for your unique child.

Chapter 3: The Strong Kids, Healthy Kids Eating Plan illustrates how the right kinds of foods, along with strength training, lead to the fastest success in improving fitness and health. Again, if you have a young child, simply implement the plan by offering only the right foods to your child. Older children can read the book for themselves and will need your help in keeping the house stocked with the appropriate foods and beverages.

And you don't have to do this alone. Sign on to my free, interactive Web blog www.seriousstrength.yuku.com to engage me and others who are on the same ship we call family. Together, we can raise stronger, healthier kids.

For more information about the Strong Kids, Healthy Kids program, please visit the following websites and web forums: www.SeriousStrength.com. and www.StrongkidsHealthyKids.com.

C H A P T E R

The Slow Speed Training Program Basics

"Slow and steady wins the race."
—Anonymous

When it comes to weight lifting, resistance training, or—as I prefer to call it—*strength training* (a much more positive way of saying it for kids and adults), a truer statement could not be made. Slow and steady training with weights makes an athletic kid faster and stronger and is better for fat loss than aerobic activity. Does that surprise you?

Before I delve into the meat of this program, I want to make sure that you, as the supervising adult, have a firm grasp of the important safety issues. If you've heard that lifting weights is bad for kids, I'm about to change your mind with hard facts and proven research.

DO YOUNG KIDS HAVE THE HORMONES THEY NEED TO BUILD MUSCLE?

Some people question whether strength training makes kids require hormones for real strength gains. In other words, if kids want to gain strength, the belief is that they don't have enough natural hormones and would need to supplement. This is untrue. Researchers Dr. Jeffrey A. Guy and Dr. Lyle J. Micheli, Director of Boston Children's Hospital, found that there was no need for such supplementation and that gains in strength are largely due to increased neuromuscular activation and coordination, rather than muscle hypertrophy.[1] What this means is kids gain strength just fine without any supplementation.

The Committee on Sports Medicine and Fitness has concluded that "in addition to the obvious goal of getting stronger, strength training programs may be undertaken to improve sports performance, rehabilitate injuries, prevent injuries, and/or enhance long-term health. Studies have shown that strength training, when properly structured with regard to frequency, mode (type of lifting), intensity, and duration of program, can increase strength in preadolescents and adolescents. Strength training programs do not seem to adversely affect linear growth and do not seem to have any long-term detrimental effect on cardiovascular health." So what this means is that strength training is very safe and beneficial for your child.

There is much more evidence available that substantiates the safety and efficacy of strength training for youngsters. If you would like further proof and even more in-depth reassurance, you can refer to the Appendix on page 149 for a list of scholarly research findings.

?

DID YOU KNOW? Drinking a gallon of cool water over the course of a day will burn as many calories as jogging for a half hour on the treadmill?

HAVE REALISTIC EXPECTATIONS

Although strength training can have positive results in young athletes, it will not turn the average child into an Olympic gold medalist or a heavily muscled superhero. There are many factors that contribute to a child's ability to excel at a given sport or to have a body like a gymnast. I think it's essential for adults to realize that genetic factors limit how well a child can perform and the body the child will ultimately grow into. Strength training will help your child to be stronger, more fit, and move closer toward being the best athlete that he or she is able to be within a natural range of possibilities. And that is the best goal to strive for.

After beginning the program, your child's strength gains will be quite dramatic from the strength training program. From one week to the next, your child will feel his or her strength building and you will need to increase the weight regularly, meaning at just about every workout session. Once your child is stronger and better conditioned, his or her improvement will slow. This is normal.

The reason is that most of the initial gains in strength are neurological. What this means is the child is simply learning how to do something new. For example, when a child or an adult learns a new skill, like ice skating, it takes time for the brain to learn how the skill must be coordinated. There is a lot of wobbling and falls can happen until the brain, nerves, and muscles get it together, so to speak. This takes time and the time it takes is very individual. Although ice skating is arguably harder to learn than a push-up, a push-up is still a skill that has to be learned. So when a child learns to do simple exercises that have never been done before, strength gains come pretty quickly because—session by session—as the child becomes better at the skill, more muscle fibers are innervated (used). After a period of about six to eight weeks, these gains in strength slow because the skill is no longer the issue. Now, real muscle and bone are being built and this is a slow and gradual process.

You won't visibly see much change (meaning bigger muscles) on the body of a child who has not yet reached puberty unless there is a good deal of fat to lose. So even though the strength is improving dramatically in a leaner child, you will not see big, bulging muscles. Their hormones are still too "young," so physical changes are fewer than when they grow into their teens. Although less dramatic, physical changes still occur. And the strength they gain is still useable strength that allows them to play better, to burn more calories, and to improve their body composition.

Teenagers, on the other hand, may experience a more dramatic change in appearance. Don't be too surprised after a couple of months if your skinny 16-year-old has bulging biceps or your heavy 14-year-old melts into a lithe and strong young lass. It's possible with strength training and it's a wonderful thing to see.

• • •

Every child has a different idea of what it means to be a good athlete. Although parents, coaches, and trainers have their own ways of motivating a child to excel at a sport, simply supporting in whatever the child is doing goes a long way in keeping that child committed to a sport.

In our zeal as parents, we sometimes get caught up in the desire to pressure and to make unrealistic expectations— sometimes to the point of making the child feel guilty. The very fact that kids are interested and involved in athletics is a blessing. Our job is to carefully (and with a clear understanding of our children's need to please us) guide them toward what they want and enjoy.

You need to help your child realize that improvement, as well as the enjoyment of the game or sport, is the main goal. Understanding the rules and regulations of the sport that your child is involved in is important. Often, it is not the strongest or most athletically gifted children who excel, but rather the children who have a deep and thorough understanding of the rules and principles of a game. And spending time learning these rules together makes for special moments. I remember teaching my daughter Georgia how to play baseball, to learn the rules, to think about the game was very rewarding for both of us.

So nurture your child not with high expectations but through enjoyment, effort, and teamwork. In this way, each child will perform to his or her own gifts. This is not to say that healthy competition should be avoided and that the desire to win should not be encouraged. Winning is a good thing and it teaches many positive aspects of how to succeed in adulthood. It's how we win, not that we win, that matters most.

ARE TWO 20-MINUTE SESSIONS REALLY ENOUGH?

The beauty of strength training is its potency. Only two 20-minute strength training sessions a week bestow on kids all the benefits that strength training provides adults. Research has shown that even *one* weekly strength training session produces almost 70 percent of the benefits of twice weekly training. This is a tremendous boon for busy parents.

Everything you've heard about exercise having to be done nearly daily to be beneficial is simply not true. Your forehead might be a touch wrinkled right now or you might be sporting a raised eyebrow as you wonder *how can this be*? Let me explain.

The act of strength training is nothing more than a *stimulus*—a spark that initiates the metabolic processes that result in larger, stronger, and more enduring muscles as well as all of the benefits associated with strength training. The result of the stimulus occurs not *while* you are exercising but afterward. Think of it this way—you don't become healthier *as* you exercise, you get stronger as you *recover* from exercise.

This is why you do not need as much exercise as the fitness industry (who would like you to buy as much of their products as possible) would have you believe.

In fact, exercise can actually be detrimental if it is performed too often. It's like lying outside in the summer sun with the intention of looking like a swimsuit model. Too much sun is dangerous and can lead to more than just a sunburn. The same is true for strength training: More is *not* better. Strength training is the spark that ignites the strengthening flame. Once ignited, this flame will last for several days and then start to wane. You then, after several days, strength train once again and continue this process as the months and years roll by. If your training sessions are too close together or too frequent, you don't allow the muscles and the nervous system enough time to fully recover. When this happens, you don't get the full—or possibly any—benefits from your exercise efforts. This situation is known as *overtraining.* Overtraining can lead to sleeplessness, irritability, a loss of appetite. and a host of other unwanted effects.

Research conducted by Wayne Westcott and Avery Faigenbaum over the last decade tell us that two weekly strength training sessions are just as beneficial as three. Research also indicates that more than three strength training sessions offer no additional benefits. Research also indicates that one weekly session produces most of the benefits of twice weekly training and, over time, produces the same results. For young athletes who are involved in lots of sports practice, one session seems to be better than two. And the reason for this is *recovery.* When a muscle is exercised, it undergoes stress. This stress causes the muscle to be depleted of its resources and also causes microscopic damage. Although a pinprick is small, it takes time for it to heal. The same thing must be allowed to happen to your muscles. Although the damage is microscopic, it still takes time to heal. You can't feel it and you can't see it, but it is real and you and your child need adequate recovery to reap the rewards of resistance (strength) training!

WHAT YOU SHOULD KNOW ABOUT FLEXIBILITY AND STRETCHING

It's a nice feeling to wake up in the morning and stretch your arms, back, and legs. It is so soothing and relaxing when we do this. I love to watch my kids wake up in the morning and see them go through their stretching routines. But let me ask you this: when we wake up and perform this almost instinctual ritual, are we really stretching? Not really. What we're really doing when we wake up and pull our elbows and head back is contracting the muscles of the back and neck. This contraction sends blood into the muscles of the back and neck and causes a soothing and wonderful feeling. It is an active contraction of your muscles, not a passive stretching of the joints, which is what traditional stretching usually is.

We've all heard that stretching is good for us so often that it has become gospel. The fact is, however, that there is really no such thing as *muscular flexibility.* A bold and confusing statement, I realize, but let's look at the facts.

Muscles are organs that are made up of groups of fibers that shorten and lengthen—or contract and uncontract—as the *joint* flexes and extends. Joints possess flexibility, while muscles possess contractility. Performing stretching exercises in order to make the muscles more flexible is like pulling on a door to make it open wider. If you pull hard enough all you'll wind up doing is damaging the hinges (the joint of the door) and perhaps the door itself.

But why is it that when people stretch, after a time they can seemingly move their joints throughout a greater range of motion? Several different studies conducted by various researchers across the globe have come to similar conclusions. When people engage in stretching programs, the contractile properties of the *muscle* do not change, which means the muscles do not experience any direct benefit. Instead, the subjects in these studies became more tolerant to the discomfort of the stretching.[2–5]

You can try this out for yourself. Sit on the floor and straighten your legs completely. Sit up as tall as possible and slowly, while keeping your back arched and rigid, try and touch your toes. As you stretch farther and farther, you'll soon feel a deep discomfort in the back of your thighs—but don't push past this point! If you did this stretch day in and day out for several weeks, you would eventually get used to the feeling and be able to stretch farther. This is called stretch tolerance and it is simply that—a tolerance of the stretch. You have not created longer or more pliable muscles (this is the little white lie Pilates practitioners tell us). All you have done is become accustomed to the feeling.

Now I know that a lot of coaches and trainers advocate stretching, especially for kids involved in sports, and I know it seems as if it is a good thing for kids to do, but there is no scientific evidence or any theoretical basis for stretching. In fact, if you stretch too much, you can damage the ligaments that attach bones together. Ligaments have little blood flow and when lengthened, they are lengthened *permanently*. This may be necessary if you are a dancer or a martial artist, but it is not healthy. In fact, several studies have shown that athletes' power output is *decreased* when they stretch as it can loosen ligaments and tendons to the point where less force can be developed, like an old and worn-out rubber band. So if your child is involved in a sport that requires explosive power (e.g., football, wrestling, sprinting, and so forth) stretching may very well be counterproductive.[6]

When kids become stronger, they are better able to move a joint throughout a greater range of motion. They will be able to perform any joint motion better because the underlying muscles are better able to move the joint and better able to stabilize and protect the joint from injury. Many research papers on the subject bear this out. We know that strength training improves joint range of motion in adults. There is no reason to believe that it will not do the same (if necessary) for kids.

We often use the term *stretching* in the wrong context. To use the same example, a child wakes up in the morning and pulls his or her elbows back, thereby stretching the muscles of the chest. But is the child actually doing this? What happens is that by pulling the elbows back, the muscles of the back are contracting and thus the muscles of the chest stretch. What this child (or the adult for that matter) is doing is squeezing and contracting the muscles of the back. So rather than call this stretching, it should be called *contracting!* Powerfully contracting your muscles through strength training is the best way to increase muscular strength, which will enhance joint flexibility. Things are not always what they seem. It's one of the reasons we should let exercise science—and not exercise tradition—guide our health and fitness endeavors. A joint should never be made more flexible without a concomitant (simultaneous) increase in the strength of the muscles that surround it. So the bottom line is that there is no need to stretch before or after a strength training program. Furthermore, the act of stretching to increase safety or to improve athletic performance should be heavily considered. Having said all this, I know that a lot of people still like to stretch and feel good when they do. If stretching is something that makes you feel good, then by all means do it—but carefully. Kids, however, do not need to stretch before or after athletic endeavors.

WHAT YOU SHOULD KNOW ABOUT SPORT-SPECIFIC TRAINING

Sport-specific training (SST) is growing in popularity today more than ever. SST uses techniques such as balancing devices, explosive jumping called plyometrics, and various sprinting movements (often with weights attached to the body and off boxes of various heights) as well as other drills in order, it is claimed, to develop speed, agility, and power in or for a given sport. Although it seems as if this training could be beneficial, these types of programs actually contribute little to improved *transfer* to specific athletic performance and can be harmful. Now, I tell you about this because I care about the health and athletic success of your child. I do not want your child to fall prey to what I like to call "innocent ignorance." I've met many caring and wonderful coaches and trainers who were simply unaware that these practices violate motor learning principles and potentially lead athletes toward unnecessary injury for no added benefit to their sports performance.

I know this will raise the hackles of some coaches and trainers, but there is merit to what I am saying here. I do not intend to insult or to patronize—not in the least. So, please bear with me here as it is important as a parent, coach, or trainer to understand this concept.

Although dozens of organizations promote sport-specific training, the issue of sport specificity is a misunderstood concept. In his book *Motor Learning and Performance,* Richard A. Schmidt, Ph.D., writes (the words in brackets are mine to help clarify):

> A common misconception is that fundamental abilities [running, jumping, balancing, etc.] can be trained through various drills or other activities.... For example, athletes are often given various "quickening" exercises, with the hope that these exercises would train some fundamental ability to be quick, allowing quicker response in their particular sports. Coaches [as well as physical therapists, athletic trainers, and personal trainers] often use various balancing drills to increase general balancing ability, eye movement exercises to improve vision, and many others. Such attempts to train fundamental abilities may sound fine, but usually they simply do not work.
>
> There are two correct ways to think of these principles. First, there is no general ability to be quick, to balance, or to use vision. Rather, quickness, balance, and vision are each based on many diverse abilities, so there is no single quick-

ness or balance ability, for example, that can be trained. [What Dr. Schmidt means here, for example, is that there is no such thing as balance, per se. If a sport or skill requires you to be good at balancing, say on a balance beam, you must practice on the balance beam. Standing on a balance ball to develop your balance on the balance beam will do little to no good even though it may be harder to do and learn. You'll just get better balancing on the ball.]

Second, even if there were such general abilities, these are, by definition, genetic and not subject to modification through practice. [Here Dr. Schmidt is not saying that good form and technique is not important. On the contrary. What he is saying is that superior vision or balance is something you are born with.] Therefore, attempts to modify a specific ability with a nonspecific drill are ineffective. A learner may acquire additional skill at the drill which is, after all, a skill itself, but this learning does not transfer to the main skill of interest.

In short, it is a mistake to try and mimic a sport skill by altering the specific skill in some fashion. The best way to enhance performance in activities such as running bases, slapping the hockey puck into the net, or shooting basketball foul shots is to practice these skills exactly as you will perform them in play.

The reason why kids and adults alike sometimes experience improvements in their sport when they engage in these sorts of practices is because they result, however inadvertently, in *increased muscular strength.* It is fairly well established (and obvious from sports players who lift weights and, unfortunately, use illegal substances to develop super strength) that improvements in muscular strength transfer to improvements in athletic endeavors to various different degrees. Additionally, proponents of SST programs usually include general strength training in the training of their athletes, so again this is the main reason why athletic prowess increases. Per individual, greater strength (and skill) equals greater performance.[7]

Of course, the bottom line is safety. As fun as they may be, there is not much physiological benefit to your child in these types of practices and, due to the potential risks—for example, sprained ankles from jumping off high boxes, torn knee cartilage from sudden twisting, and spinning drills to improve agility, and so on—my advice is to stay away from them altogether. Injury sustained while playing the actual sport is one thing—these are inevitable and par for the course. But injuries that occur for no good reason due to performing activities that offer no scientifically proven athletic benefit should not be tolerated.

The better solution for improved sports performance is controlled strength training, which can greatly improve strength and endurance along with the specific and exact practice of the necessary skills. The bottom line is that practice makes perfect, but only if the practice is perfect to begin with! And for practice to be "perfect," the exact skill—not a similar or altered way of performing the skill—should be practiced. If running the bases is a skill that needs improving, the athlete is best served by running regulation bases, not running around different-size cones (a common practice for improving agility around the bases). If a hockey player needs to improve her slap shots, she should put on her gear and get on the ice and practice slap shots, not toss the medicine ball with sudden and explosive spine-twisting drills to increase her slap shot power.

WHAT YOU SHOULD KNOW ABOUT FITNESS TESTS

In my opinion, fitness tests are essentially useless for assessing a child's physical fitness. They can also be psychologically counterproductive. Fitness tests like the ones that are commonplace in schools and camps are designed to give a general idea as to whether a child is physically fit. These tests come in many different forms. The usual ones include but are not limited to how many jumping jacks, push-ups, or sit-ups a child can perform in a given time frame to assess strength and muscular endurance, a sit-and-reach test to determine flexibility, and a step-up test (a step-up test is when you step up and down on a high platform or stair, alternating legs, for a certain period of time) or shuttle runs (running laps back and forth a certain distance in a certain time frame) to determine cardiorespiratory robustness.

Organizations like the American College of Sports Medicine set specific guidelines for these tests. Unfortunately for many kids, they do not take into account the child's body proportions, overall size, and perhaps most important their desire to take the test. Take the sit-and-reach test, for example. A child is supposed to sit down on the floor with legs straightened and reach forward to see how close he can come to touching his toes or hit a specific marker of inches. If the child has long legs, a short torso, and short arms (and perhaps a touch too much belly fat to boot), he won't come close to touching his toes or making the minimum required inches. So he is deemed inflexible or tight when that is not at all the case. The proportions of his body disallow him to score positively on the test, which does not take body proportions into account. (Remember earlier we learned that muscular flexibility is not a real thing.) So, it's a senseless test from the start.

The same misinterpretation (meaning that the test for flexibility actually measures something useful) happens when an overfat child tries to do push-ups or chin-ups. She'll have a hard time doing even one chin-up or push-up but it is her body weight not her lack of strength that is the issue. Fitness tests can easily discourage a child if he or she doesn't fare well and set the child up for ridicule and unnecessary cruelty by peers. I recognize that many schools have devised ways to lessen these discouragements and that is a good thing. But are these tests really necessary at all? In my opinion, they are not and the time would be better spent on strength training.

Fitness tests are entirely different from setting goals. Goal setting is a great way to motivate children to achieve. Of course, the goal must be realistic and something that you and your child discuss and agree on together. I am not attempting to tell you how or what to do. This is up to you, the coach, or the teacher. I am merely pointing out the difference to avoid confusion.

At Serious Strength, we often set goals in small increments. For example, if a child performs an exercise using 50 pounds and completes 10 repetitions, the next time he comes in, we'll add 1 or 2 pounds and try to achieve 10 repetitions again. At each session, the child will make progress in his strength in most exercises either by lifting more weight or doing more repetitions—or both.

I believe realistic and incremental goal setting when strength training a child to be very uplifting, motivating, and fun!

The Slow Speed Exercises

I will describe three different strength training routines for you:

1. Home-based routine (which can also be modified for schools/gym classes)

2. Gym-based routine

It's nice to have the choice between these different programs since you never know where you'll be or what your child prefers. A gym-based routine will always be superior to a playground- or home-based routine unless you have quality equipment in your home. It's much easier to make steady and gradual weight progressions in a gym with calibrated equipment. Also, in a gym environment there are fewer distractions like the TV, friends calling, and so forth. But this does not mean the home or program won't work.

I've tried to make the exercises very simple and doable. You'll see that the explanations are clear and easy to follow. You don't need to understand all of the technical trivia of strength training to help your child.

When it comes to strength training, as with anything else meaningful in life, being consistent is the key to success. What is important is that your child does at least one session a week (two or three at the very most).

TERMS YOU NEED TO KNOW

It's a good idea to familiarize yourself with certain terms so that you can explain them to your children as they perform the exercises (and so that you know what you're doing when you strength train for yourself). You've probably already heard of some of them before.

The Repetition

A *repetition,* or rep, is the act of lifting and lowering a weight all the way up and then all the way down once. It is the period of time you spend contracting the target muscle. In order to spark a growth/strength response, meaning stronger muscles and bones, you should perform multiple repetitions with 70 percent to 80 percent of the heaviest weight you can lift only one time. Research indicates that this percentage of weight lifted (ideally until the muscles being worked are thoroughly exhausted) is a universally productive level of weight to use.

The Set

Multiple repetitions performed without a break are called a *set.*
How many reps will be in a set is determined by the amount
of weight chosen and the speed of the repetitions. The heavier
the weight or resistance, the shorter the set will last. The lighter
the weight, the longer the set will last. The slower you perform
a repetition, the fewer total repetitions you will need to do in
a set. The faster the repetitions, the more repetitions you will
need to do. We'll talk more on this topic later in the chapter.

Putting a Set Together   Research indicates that for a set to
be productive, the minimum amount of time it should take for
a set to be completed should be approximately 40 seconds
and the maximum 90 seconds (there are rare exceptions).
My recommendation is to perform the repetition in a 5-second
upward motion and a 5-second downward motion. The minimum number of repetitions will be 4 and the maximum number
of repetitions will be 9. I say maximum number of reps to
indicate that if 9 repetitions can be completed, it is time to
make the weight heavier or make the exercise more challenging. And if 4 repetitions cannot be performed, then the weight
should be made lighter.

It is better to keep the repetitions on the higher side for
kids, more toward the 90-second range, so that the exercise
doesn't seem too difficult. This instills children with a sense
of confidence and accomplishment. If the exercises feel too
demanding in the beginning, children can become discouraged.
When starting out, it is fine to make the exercises easier or
lighter and allow for upward of 2 minutes for a set to complete,
meaning, 15 repetitions or more. Over time, most youngsters
will tolerate the feeling of a challenging exercise set or session
very well. As they become more accustomed to the exercises
and the feeling of demanding work, they can make the weights
heavier or the exercise more taxing so that the set ends within
the more ideal 40- to 90-second time frame.

A GENERAL PRIMER ON HOW TO PERFORM THE EXERCISES

Warming Up

You and your child's bodies are kept at a fairly constant 98.6 degrees, so you do not need to warm up for this workout. The first few repetitions of each exercise will serve as the most perfect warm-up for the area that is being worked. So with Slow Burn training the warm-up is built right in!

Setting a Tempo

Before I describe each exercise for each program, here are the general guidelines for repetition speed, or tempo, that apply to every exercise. Take 3 seconds for the first 1 inch of movement to keep from starting too fast. Starting too quickly, as most people do in typical gyms, causes sudden and excessive forces that can result in injury. Starting slowly also makes the muscles do all of the work all of the time rather than relying on momentum. Momentum is the enemy of quality muscle work when you're exercising to develop your strength.

After the slow start, the lifting portion should be completed in roughly 7 seconds (could be a second or so longer or shorter depending on a person's limb length or the stroke length of the exercise). Don't get overly caught up in a perfect amount of seconds. Once the lift (the raising of the weight) is completed, you carefully reverse direction in approximately 3 seconds and continue (lower) in approximately 7 seconds.

What this means is that the *entire repetition may take as long as 20 seconds (or longer) to complete.* The length of time, however, is not a hard-and-fast rule as it depends on the exercise you are performing.

For example, your legs are longer than your arms (I hope!). Performing an exercise for your arms will take less time to complete since the distance is shorter. So when you do an arm exercise, the time it takes to complete a repetition will usually be less than a similar exercise for the legs.

The key is to start very slowly, taking 3 seconds to begin the exercise, which causes less force at the outset, and then moving slowly and steadily after that.

To make it a touch simpler for young kids, they can perform each exercise in a 5 second up, 5 second down count, or 10 total seconds per complete repetition. It's a lot easier to remember and execute. Counting to five is a simple thing to do for any kid and the difference in outcome is negligible.

If your child is still young and is into action heroes, princesses, or superhero characters, you can be creative and count in different languages or use the names of their favorite characters to make it a lot more fun. Instead of counting numbers, you could say "Spiderman, Superman, Batman, Aquaman, Daredevil!" When we train kids, we don't always use these characters. It's something that you should investigate with your own child or children to use as a tool to make it fun and interesting to them.

So, it should take approximately 5 seconds to finish saying the names, or counting, then the child reverses direction, and you repeat the names or whatever you're using again. It's a little more fun like this for youngsters than just counting 1, 2, 3, 4, 5.

Finding Your Range of Motion

Each exercise should be performed throughout the greatest, pain-free range of motion as possible. That means you should never fully extend or lock out your joints. For example, if you are performing an exercise for the biceps (which is a hinge type of joint), the arms should start with the elbows slightly bent rather than completely straight. Completely straightening your arm can sometimes irritate a joint and cause some tenderness. It's better to start slightly bent and then move toward a fully bent (meaning contracted) position.

For joints that are the ball-and-socket type (e.g., shoulder and hip), you need to start from a position that is slightly less than what the child can naturally stretch into. So for each child, the range of motion will be slightly different. The most important thing to keep in mind is that the exercise, from start to finish, should be performed in a pain-free fashion.

Breathing

Always encourage your child to breathe freely. The rule with breathing is this: Breathe! Holding the breath should always be avoided because it causes blood pressure to rise unnecessarily. The medical term for holding the breath is *valsalva.* To control valsalva, simply breathe **more.** Tell your child to huff and puff like a train or try to blow out a hundred candles on a birthday cake. Sometimes overbreathing (hyperventilation) can cause a little dizziness but it isn't harmful. I know that many of you have heard to breathe in on the lift and out on the lowering. Some experts suggest the opposite, in fact. This recommendation does not take into account the speed or tempo that you are using to lift and lower weights. When lifting in a slow rep fashion, this would be a bit difficult to do—they'd be some pretty long breaths. The point is that you breathe freely at all times and not hold your breath. This is the most important takeaway concept.

Maintaining Posture

For each exercise I've described what posture or form the child should strive to keep. Do your best to follow the recommendations and photos in this book. Show your child the pictures of the kids in this book doing the exercise and get him or her to mimic the postures in the photographs as closely as possible. It's much easier for children of any age to understand what you want them to do when they can see a visual to guide them. Always stress good form to children rather than how much weight they lift. Praise them for keeping their bodies in the proper position more than for how many reps they've performed. This is very important for the younger tykes.

Wearing Proper Attire

When strength training, it's best to wear clothes that allow for body heat to escape. Keeping cool is an important part of maximizing your child's ability to work hard. A T-shirt and shorts is the best garb to train in, but whatever is comfortable works. Sneakers or other non-heeled, soft-soled shoes are the choice for footwear. I don't suggest bare feet even when doing the home program. All it takes is for a weight to mistakenly fall on a toe. So keep the shoes on. But when you are doing the push-ups or the body weight squats, it's okay to do them in bare feet.

WHAT KIDS HAVE TO SAY

"What I like about strength training is the way I feel after training and the way my muscles feel during the workout."
—**Georgia, age 8**

Muscular Success

Each exercise should be performed until no further repetitions are possible in good form for that particular exercise. This means that the muscles being worked are as *totally exhausted* as the child can tolerate. In the exercise business it's called *training to muscular failure.*

The word *failure* is not the most positive-sounding word in the English language. It conjures up poor performance and missed opportunities: "I failed to score the winning goal." Or "I failed to complete my assignment." But in strength training, failure is great. In fact, it's success. Here's why.

All muscles of the body are composed of fibers, like strings on an instrument. Whenever you flex a joint (e.g., bend an elbow), you contract a muscle. The fibers of that muscle are called into play and the joint moves. You literally have thousands of muscle fibers throughout each muscle. When you exercise, your brain communicates with the muscle fibers through the nerves and says, "contract and move." But the brain will only call on the minimum necessary amount of fibers to do the job. Easy exercises like walking call for very few fibers to be used. It is one of the reasons why you can walk for a long time and the main reason why walking is not the most effective form of exercise for improving the human body. Yes, a pleasant stroll is enjoyable, unlikely to cause injury, and can be a great way to reduce stress, but for improving the health of your body, it sits fairly low on the exercise totem pole.

When the demands on your muscles grow stronger— for example, when you ride a bike up a very steep hill—more and more fibers are called on to come and help. If the demands are so great that even after all of the fibers are called up, the muscle cannot continue to perform the exercise, muscle failure has been reached. If this happens when you are riding your bike, then your bike ride is no fun. If this were to happen when swimming, the lifeguard would have to be summoned. We don't want muscle failure during recreational activities, but you *do* want it when you strength train. When the muscle is worked hard enough to fail in an exercise, you have succeeded in *ensuring* that you are creating a stronger muscle. It's success through failure.

PARENT TO PARENT

Shortly after Katya and Marc started their program at Serious
Strength, my expectations that Fred would provide an effective,
professional, and safe workout for my children were confirmed.
Katya's Junior Prep figure skating program coach wanted to know
what Katya did so that almost overnight her jumps became so
considerably stronger. On the same night, I talked to Katya's ballet
teacher, who could not believe that all of a sudden Katya made
such a breakthrough in flexibility. As for Marc, not only did his
hockey power skating improve very fast, but I can actually see
how his muscles have grown. And the other day, I discovered
that without any additional training Marc can do military-style
pull-ups—a huge ego booster for both Marc—and his parents!
    —**Veronica and Yakov B.**

Like anything else new, this deep muscle fatigue at first
will feel odd and a little funny to children. It will also feel a
bit uncomfortable. Over time, however, they'll get used to it.
How long it takes varies from child to child. Most of our kids
take to the feeling after the first few sessions and come to
like it very much. They find the feeling of gooey arms and
rubbery legs really funny and get a kick out of it! Older children,
just like adults, will come to associate this feeling with the
knowledge that they've had a successful workout.

I call the moment the child reaches this point *muscular
success.* It's a good idea to say, "success!" out loud because
for younger kids it's important to always reinforce their accomplishments. My daughter likes it when I say, "outstanding!"

?

Some instructors at Serious Strength use different phrases to praise the success point. Tommy Day likes to say, 'YTTNL!'" (*You took it to the next level!*) and then give a high five. This is better for older kids but you get the idea. Kids of all ages can't get enough of real, honest praise and encouragement. But I do stress *honest* praise. Kids are smart—they'll smell an empty compliment a mile away. If a child doesn't work as hard as you know he could or his form is not quite as clean as it could be, you absolutely should address this situation and work to better it in a positive manner. We are always showing kids (and adults) correct form and ways to think about keeping their focus. "Let me hear you breathe like a steam train!" "Pretend you're a statue and only your arms (or legs) can move."

THE HOME OR SCHOOL GYM ROUTINE

The home exercise routine consists of five basic exercises designed to strengthen the entire body either directly or indirectly. The muscles of the body work synergistically, so when you are targeting a specific muscle such as your chest, other muscles must also tense and contract. This is why you don't need to perform dozens of distinct exercises to get a good overall strengthening effect. The only "more" you need to worry about is more focus, more intensity of effort, and more consistency—not "more" exercise.

One caveat: children who are very overfat will have a much harder time performing strength exercises that use their body weight as the resistance. When a child is heavy, body weight provides more resistance than they can lift and lower for certain exercises such as push-ups. It will be necessary for you to assess your child in these circumstances, and more than likely it will require a small financial investment in some weights, a bench, and some other items (that you'll be able to use, too). A description of each item and where to find it is on pages 151–152.

Here is the at-home routine and the muscles that are strengthened by each exercise:

- Squats (quadriceps, hamstring, and gluteus muscles, aka front and back of legs and the buttocks)

- Floor push-ups (pectorals, triceps, and deltoid muscles, aka chest, shoulders, back of the arms)

- Single arm pull-ups (latissimus dorsi and biceps, aka the back and front of the arms)

- Floor crunches (abdominal muscles, aka stomach)

- Water jug or dumbbell shoulder raises (deltoid and trapezius muscles, aka shoulders)

- Overhead shoulder press (same as the shoulder raises including the triceps, aka back of the arms)

Home Equipment

You need the following tools available for the home program:

- Two gallon-size water jugs or adjustable dumbbells ranging in weight from 1 pound to 20 pounds

- Three towels or an exercise mat

- Workout chart and a pencil (see Appendix for the Strong Kids Progress Chart)

- Jump rope

- Sturdy stool

- Fan

- Repetition counter (see Appendix)

- Metronome (see Appendix)

The water jugs or dumbbells will be used for the one arm pull-ups and for the side lateral raises. They can also be used when body weight doorknob squats become too easy.

The towel or mat is used for doing the push-ups and floor crunches on hard surfaces. If you already have a nice soft rug or carpet then you may not need these items.

The jump rope is used in the crunches in the event that the child is too weak to do a sit-up with his or her body weight. It can be tied around the doorknob and used to help rise upward and then released as the downward motion begins.

The chart and the pencil are to keep accurate records of each training session so that you know precisely when to increase the resistance or to change the way the exercise is performed to make it more difficult.

The fan is entirely optional. It is a lot easier to perform strengthening exercises if the air is moving and the room is cool. Sweating is a sign of overheating and is to be avoided as best as possible. If sweating occurs, this means the body is trying to cool itself down and the ability to exercise and to concentrate diminishes.

The metronome is used to help keep the beat or tempo of the slow speed. You can buy one online or at a music store for approximately $20 or less. (See the equipment resources section in the Appendix.). You simply set the tempo to 60 beats per second. Explain to your child that each beat is 1 second and since we are doing the exercises at a 5-second up and a 5-second down count (or slower), it should take 5 beats of the metronome to lift and 5 to lower. Slower than 5 up and 5 down is certainly okay.

Be sure to pick the correct weight, and keep cool.

Rest Between Exercises

The exercises can be performed one right after the other or, if preferred, with a minute rest period between them. There is no hard science on the benefit of either and I find in my experience that results come either way. The best thing to do is to give enough time to feel unrushed and to make sure that the exercises are set up correctly.

WORKOUT PROGRESS CHART

The workout progress chart is designed to keep track of your repetitions and the weights used so that you can accurately judge your progress. It is fairly self-explanatory, but in short, place the name of the exercise in the first column called Name of Exercise. In the second column, place the seat and other settings for the machines. You can also place any notes about either workout in this section as well. The third column is used for weight used and the order of the exercise. So if the first exercise is the leg press, write the weight used in the top of the triangle and the number 1 in the lower triangle. Reps completed is of course the number of repetitions completed for that exercise.

THE EXERCISES

SQUATS

Muscles Targeted: quadriceps, hamstrings, and buttocks

Setup

Equipment: Dumbbells or jugs of water

Stand with feet shoulder width apart and with arms in front of the body held out straight. The arms held out help to counterbalance the child's weight so that she can squat down far enough (hips slightly below the knees) without feeling as if she'll fall over forward.

Adjust the fan, if needed, so that it blows on the body, but not in the eyes, because watering eyes will break the child's concentration. Keep the feet/toes slightly in front of the knees to avoid putting pressure on the knees.

Breathing should be easy and relaxed throughout the exercise. You don't want any breath holding, teeth gritting, or grimacing. The focus should be on the muscles of the buttocks and thighs as they work smoothly through the movement. It is best to press mainly through the heels as the child performs the exercise. Don't let the heels rise off the floor. The knees should always stay just behind the toes.

1. Slowly begin to lower to the count of 5, keeping the knees behind toes. Once the hips are below the knee, reverse slowly and begin to rise upward on the count of 5 until the knees are almost completely straight (but not quite).

Start/Finish Position

Halfway/Endpoint

2. This is one complete repetition. Count out loud "One!" or "Superman!" or "Uno!"

3.   Begin to lower and then rise upward again. That's the second rep—count it out loud again.

4.   Continue the squat repetitions in this manner until no further repetitions are possible in good form. Record the number of repetitions completed and move on to the next exercise.

5.   Words of encouragement at this point are essential. Kids love to hear they've done a great job, so tell your child, "Outstanding effort!" In my experience, you can't give too much genuine approval.

Make sure your child adheres to the range of motion and the 5/5 repetition speed. Very often kids (and adults) speed up, lock their knees straight at the top to rest, and shorten the range of motion, which makes the exercise easier. Make sure you're keeping the exercise pure.

Making the Exercise Easier

If the squats are too hard, possibly because the child's body weight is too high, the child can do the exercise while holding on to a doorknob and use his arms to help pull himself up and then, without the use of the arms, lower back down. The downward motion should be no problem for almost any child. As strength gains occur little by little, the child can use his arms less and less and then eventually not use the door to help.

Making the Exercise Harder

If the body weight squats are too easy, there are two ways to make the exercise more demanding. The first thing is to slow the repetitions. Try slowing the repetition speed to 7 seconds or longer and record this change in the notes section in the workout chart. You can also fill the gallon water jugs and do the squats holding the water jugs or the dumbbells. The water jugs add resistance to the child's body weight and make the exercise more challenging.

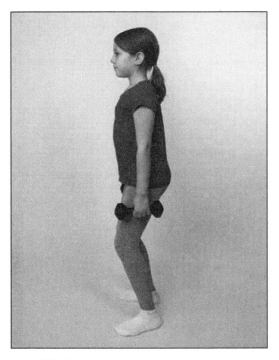

Start/Finish Position

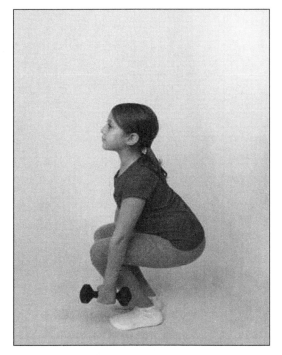

Halfway/Endpoint

FLOOR PUSH-UPS

Muscles Targeted: pectorals, triceps, deltoid

Setup

Equipment: Three towels (or an exercise mat if your child prefers) if you feel you need these for comfort on the knees and hands.

Fold the towels so that they are thick and place one on the floor in front of where your child's forehead will touch the ground. Put the other two for the knees under each knee. If the floor surface is slippery, forget the towels as you don't want them to slip out from underneath the child.

    Have your child kneel on the towels and place his hands, shoulder width apart, on the floor in line with his armpits. His knees should be shoulder width as well. He should hold his body steady in the start position with elbows slightly bent and back as straight as an ironing board. The chin should stay tucked in a bit about a fist's distance from the chest to prevent excessive arching of the neck.

1. *Slowly* have the child begin to lower smoothly until the forehead reaches the towel in 5 seconds (counting, "Baseball! Football! Hockey! Basketball! Soccer!"). Once his forehead touches the towel, the direction should be reversed slowly and gradually without stopping or resting even for a second. Count in the same fun way again on the upward motion.

Start/Finish Position

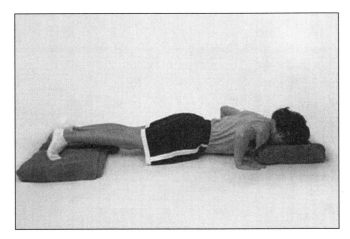

Halfway/Endpoint

2. Take 5 full seconds to push back up, moving a few inches per second. Continue pressing upward until the straight-arm position is reached, but *not locked* at the elbows. This is one completed repetition. Count out "one!" and click the repetition counter or make a mark on your chart so as not to forget.

3. *Slowly* reverse direction again, continuing until the child is unable to complete another rep without breaking perfect form by jerking, thrusting, or resting. Record the number of repetitions.

Words of encouragement and praise at this point are in order. ("I'll bet Superman couldn't have done that!")

Making the Exercise Easier

To make the exercise easier, place the knees on the towels instead of the toes, keeping the toes off the floor and perform the exercise in the same manner.

Some children, especially overfat children, might have trouble with the push-ups because they have so much body weight to move. If he is not strong enough to raise his body even once, an easier yet still effective variation is to do only

Start/Finish Position

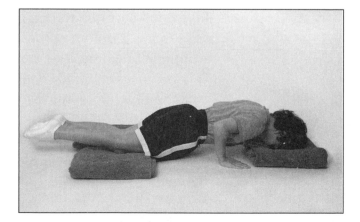

Halfway/Endpoint

the lowering portion of the rep. Once the forehead touches the towel, instruct the child to carefully sit back on the calves and heels and push up and forward to return to the starting position again. Then immediately get set and begin to slowly lower down again. He should continue to perform the lowering half of the push-up until he cannot lower his body with complete, slow control. In time, this technique will strengthen him up enough to do the full push-up.

Making the Exercise Harder

If your child is already so strong that he is unable to reach fatigue by 90 seconds (that would be one strong kid!), he's ready for seriously slow push-ups. Instead of using the 5 up/5 down counts, double this and try 10 seconds up and 10 seconds down. Such an advanced technique is *very difficult.* Make sure that your child can do the original version in very good form before you attempt to try this one or you might discourage him. You can even try an in-between number like 7 seconds to push up and let down.

If the hard version is too hard and the easy version is too easy, there is still an alternative. Let the child begin on his toes, lower slowly to where the forehead touches the towel, then let the knees touch the floor with feet off of the floor and slowly begin pushing up. When his arms are straight, he'll again straighten his knees, supporting his weight on the toes and arms and then lower again. Continue in this way until he cannot raise his forehead from the towel or lower in good form.

If your child needs to catch his breath or simply relax for a second before moving on to the next exercise, that is fine.

SINGLE ARM BACK PULL-UPS

Muscles Targeted: latissimus dorsi and biceps

Setup

Equipment: A stool and a 5-pound dumbbell or a half-filled gallon water jug. (This weight is just an estimate—every child is different and it will take some trial and error to choose the proper resistance in order to deeply fatigue the muscles within the 4- to 9-rep range that corresponds to the 40- to 90-second time frame.)

In this exercise, he'll work one arm while the other supports and stabilizes his body. Put the stool on a stable foundation (not a thick rug or carpet). If you are using a fan at this point, adjust it so that it will keep him cool.

Standing in front of the stool, his legs should be about shoulder width apart and in a split legged stance. Have him place one hand on the stool for support and then lean forward, so that his upper body is roughly at a 45-degree angle to the floor with a slight arch in the lower back—a soft C shape. He should now take the dumbbell or water jug in his other hand, letting it hang outstretched and ready to lift.

Just as in the other exercises, breathing should be relaxed and even throughout the exercise. No breath holding allowed! Remind your child to keep the muscles of the face calm and relaxed. Avoid teeth gnashing, grunting, and grimacing. Tell him "Make a face with your mouth wide open like you're seeing a ghost!"

1. *Slowly* initiate the movement, leading with the elbow, and pull the dumbbell upward in a straight line, taking 5 full counts (again counting numbers, princesses, or superheroes) to complete the movement until the hand reaches the armpit.

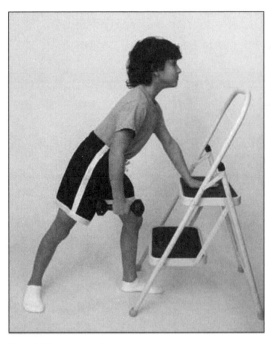

Start/Finish Position

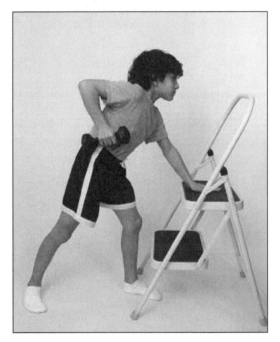

Halfway/Endpoint

2. Pause at the armpit for 2 seconds, squeezing the arm muscles as if to touch the tip of the elbow to the ceiling. Focus on the muscles of the back and upper arm as they work smoothly through the movement.

3. Then reverse direction slowly, lowering the weight until the arm is almost completely straight. Advise your child not to allow the muscles to rest by letting the arm hang in a completely straight position. Letting the weight hang

"dead" unloads the muscles and allows for rest. If you allow this to happen, the muscles will relax and we want to keep tension on the muscles at all times during the exercise.

4. Right away but *slowly* reverse direction and begin again to pull the weight up until it reaches the armpit/chest level and the tip of the elbow is toward the ceiling.

5. Continue lifting and lowering until he cannot lift the weight and still maintain perfect form and timing.

6. Now, switch to the other side and repeat this process. The other arm might be wiggly from the fatigue of the exercise so it's okay if he needs to rest a few minutes to do the other side.

7. When finished, record the repetition numbers on the chart. If the number of repetitions differ slightly this is okay. Usually the dominant arm (the one the child writes with) is stronger. It is possible that he might get one more repetition with the dominant arm than the other. (We don't see this happening a lot though.) It's not an imbalance or anything to be concerned about.

8. Give you child words of encouragement!

Making the Exercise Easier

Simply decrease the amount of weight used.

Making the Exercise Harder

Increase the amount of weight used.

STOMACH CRUNCHES

Muscles Targeted: abdominals

Setup

Equipment: Two towels (or a mat and two towels)

Have your child lie on his back on the mat or floor. The knees should be bent at approximately 90 degrees and the feet flat on the mat or the ground, hip width apart. The arms should be held straight out, as if trying to fly like a superhero. The chin should be kept tucked to the chest, not bridged backward.

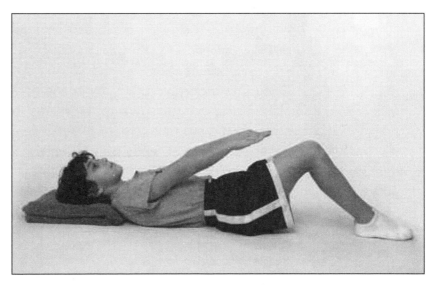

Start/Finish Position

1. *Slowly* and carefully he should begin to curl his torso upward and forward as if he is trying to touch his knees with his fingertips. The idea here is not to try and sit all the way up. Only the shoulder blades should roll up

and off the floor. The lower back should stay in contact with the towel roll.

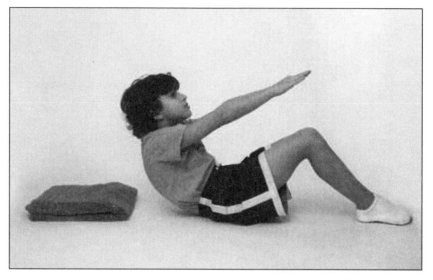

Halfway/Endpoint

2. Once the fingertips touch the knees or when they're as close as he can get them to the knees, he should pause, squeeze the stomach for a full second, and also breathe. He should try and really tighten up the stomach muscles as if a boxer was about to punch him in the gut. Tell him that!

3. After the squeeze, he should ease down *slowly,* lowering the upper torso in 5 seconds until his shoulder blades touch the floor again. At this point, the temptation to rest will be strong but *do not rest!*

4. Immediately reverse direction and begin to crunch up again.

5. It's a little bit harder to keep free and easy breathing in this exercise compared to others so encourage open and

free breathing a little more often. Try not to allow any breath holding, clenching of the teeth, grunting, grimacing, jerking, and so on.

6. Continue until success (muscle failure) is achieved.

7. Record the reps and time on the progress chart.

8. Remember to give words of praise! If he is really tuckered out, advise him to lie on the towel or mat for a while and breathe to relax.

Making the Exercise Easier

For a lot of kids straight crunches, if done properly, are very tough because the muscles of the abdomen are fairly small and weak. Some assist techniques might be necessary to perform the exercises properly.

Here are two ways to do it. First, tell your child to bring outstretched fingers a bit lower for the rising phase, so that he can touch his mid-thigh. As he crunches, he crawls up his thigh with his fingertips and lets his arms assist in the lift. Pause and squeeze just as in the routine, then let the fingertips crawl back down to almost resting.

If he still can't do the crunch, have him move over to a door, open it, and straddle it with his legs. Take the jump rope and wrap it around both doorknobs and use it to gently assist in rising to the top position. Then after a pause, lower slowly while holding the rope but without using the strength of the arms to lower back down. Eventually he will be able to do the crunches without using the arms at all.

Making the Exercise Harder

If the crunches are too easy, place the child's hands behind the head, arms relaxed, not pulling on the neck.

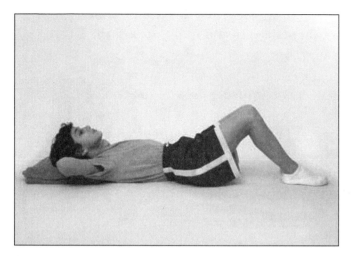

Start/Finish Position

Halfway/Endpoint

Continue doing the crunches the same way as above until
he reaches muscular success, then very quickly switch to the
easier (arms to knees) method and continue to do more
crunches until muscular success is achieved again. Using this
method, have him hold the last crunch in the crunched position,
replace his hands behind his head, and hold this position
until he cannot stop his body from lowering down.

SIDE-LATERAL SHOULDER RAISE AND SHOULDER PRESS

Muscles Targeted: Deltoids, triceps, trapezius

Setup

Equipment: Dumbbells or water jugs. Try using 5-pound dumbbells or filled water jugs at first and then experiment by going up or down in weight from there. Remember, what you're looking for is a weight that the child can correctly lift, using good form, for 4 to 9 repetitions before achieving muscular success.

Adjust the position of your fan if necessary, set your rep counter, and have chart ready.

Place the dumbbells or jugs on either side of your child's feet. Have the child bend down and grasp the weights, standing back up and letting them hang slightly away from his sides with elbows slightly bent. Have the child try and stand up straight and when doing the exercise, keep his torso from swaying to and fro or leaning from side to side.

1. Breathing should be, as always, in a relaxed, even fashion throughout the exercise. The child should avoid holding his breath, clenching his teeth, grimacing, or straining. The focus should be on the muscles of the shoulders and upper arms.

2. Slowly initiate the movement, raising the weights away from his sides smoothly. The start should be very slow to lift the weight, taking at least 5 full seconds to raise the weight to finish when the arms are parallel to the floor.

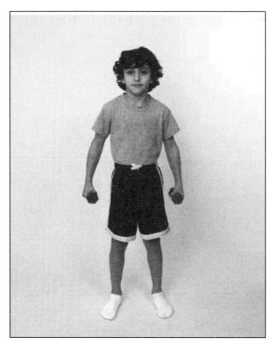

Start/Finish Position

Halfway/Endpoint

3. Pause in this position for 2 to 3 beats, then begin to
   reverse direction and slowly lower the weights, taking
   5 full counts or seconds to lower the weights smoothly
   to a point about 1 inch away from the hips. (Don't let them
   touch or rest on your hips, however.)

4. Once there, slowly reverse directions and begin to lift
   again.

5. Continue lifting and lowering smoothly until you cannot
   raise the weights away from your sides but *do not rest.*
   Move right away to the shoulder press exercise.

6. *Immediately,* but smoothly, bring the weights to shoulder height and once there, *slowly* initiate movement by pressing them overhead. Be sure to keep the dumbbells or jugs slightly in front of your face. Use the same 5-second count, stopping just short of fully straightening the arms—*don't let him lock the elbows!* (Locking the joints unloads the muscles and decreases the effectiveness of the exercise and could potentially irritate the joints.)

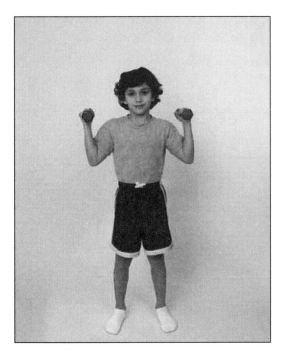

Start/Finish Position

Halfway/Endpoint

7. Once at the top of the lift, slowly reverse directions and begin to lower the weights to shoulder level, again taking 5 full seconds to reach shoulder height. Try not to let him rest the weights on his shoulders, but rather, pause briefly and reverse directions to begin another lift. Check that his body is keeping as still as possible and not swaying like a sailor on a rocky ship.

8. Continue lifting and lowering until he is no longer able raise the weights to halfway past shoulder level and record that number of repetitions. If he can complete more than 9 reps, maintaining perfect form and timing, the weight is too light and it's time to increase the weight load. Increases by 1/2 to 1 pound are best. Record the reps to failure on the workout chart.

9. Don't forget words of praise!

Making the Exercise Harder

Increase the amount of resistance as mentioned earlier.

Making the Exercise Easier

Decrease the amount of resistance. You can also have the child sit on a chair and perform the exercises in a seated fashion. The standing version is better because he'll need to use more of his core muscles to keep his body steady. But if he wobbles around, have him sit and get used to doing the exercises like this.

My stepdaughter Jillian D., during her sophomore year, was one-tenth of a second from breaking the school's record in the 200-meter run. During her off-season, Jillian incorporated Slow Burn techniques into her weight workouts. As a junior, Jillian returned to the track team stronger and faster, setting the new school record in the 200 meter. Jillian was also the anchor of the 4 × 100 relay team that not only shattered the school record in that event, but also broke their own record one week later! As a senior, Jillian has returned to her weight room strategy of again incorporating Slow Burn techniques in the hope of not only breaking more track records next spring but setting the records and standards for Kennett High's newly formed indoor track team.

—**Audley Williams**

MIGHTY TYKES AND TEENS

The truth is that children and young adults thrive on strength training. Not one child I've worked with has regretted starting on a strength training program, and all have seen benefits. All have gotten stronger, and some have even lost significant amounts of body fat. Of course, kids are not small adults. Although they have the same structure and joint-muscle functions as adults do, there are marked differences with what they can do with those muscles and joints.

There's also the issue of focus and mental involvement; the younger the child is, the greater the challenge in engaging the child in strength training. Here are some observations and challenges I've personally encountered when working with kids and young adults:

A MASTER INSTRUCTOR'S INSIGHTS

I am not the only instructor at Serious Strength who takes the kids through their training sessions. I thought it would be helpful for you to hear the experiences and opinions of other instructors who are skilled at training youngsters, especially an instructor as skilled as Eugene Thong.

Eugene is a degreed exercise physiologist and, in my opinion, one of the best instructors in the field. When it comes to training kids, his words are so right on. He says:

"I was definitely wary of the idea of training children one on one. I'd instructed children before, but in a group context and using calisthenics and play activities, not regimented strength training. Initially, I had the same misgivings as most people do when broaching the idea of training kids: Would they be disruptive? Would such a strict, rigid framework be too restricting or boring to them? For that matter, would a child even fit on the machines?"

- *Developmental issues.* Younger children (boys especially) have, at best, only fair motor control. Exercises that involve the lower body (in particular, the leg press) present a real challenge to the younger trainee in terms of control and execution. However, with practice (lots and lots of practice in some cases), virtually all kids I've worked with can attain good execution of exercises with progressing weight loads and impressive control.

- *Exercise time should be enjoyable, but not "playtime."* We've worked hard to create an air of a "serious play" space. By pre-framing the exercise floor as a place where the young trainee can have fun but is not to act up, we effectively eliminate horseplay and distractions. Knowing that the gym floor is a place to be serious but also a place of learning, of exploration, and of play, helps to properly shape the experience in their minds. It's a place where they can joke, or be friendly, but when the weight leaves the stack and enters their hands, it is a serious time.

• *How do you get a kid to work hard?* It's hard enough to make an adult (who may have far more at stake regarding improving health and minimizing pain) strength train with enough effort to stimulate changes in their body. Kids no matter what their age might not care about muscle loss, diabetes, or insulin sensitivity unless of course they have these conditions. But by and large kids don't think much about these issues. How do you get them to work hard?

One method I've found to be quite successful is to turn the session into a competition with themselves. I tell the child what he or she had done in the past, and tell them what they must do to surpass their previous performance. ("Okay, last time you got 5 reps on this exercise. Today, let's see if you can do 6 slow perfect reps.") By giving children these mini-goals to meet and beat, they get the satisfaction of making tangible progress and of taking steps toward self-mastery. Of course, there's the obligatory mini-celebration when they achieve an outstanding goal, such as the first time they can perform an exercise without assistance, or seeing an improvement in the amount of weight they lift by 20 percent.

This works particularly well with kids in small groups, as they will naturally compete with each other (especially if they are friends). I once trained a nine-year-old (we'll call him Dave) who strength trained at the same time with a friend, ten-year-old Buster. (Buster would be working with a separate instructor.) As the two of them performed the same exercises in their routines, they developed a unique interplay where Buster would set the "pace" of the workout, and Dave would try to match the pace. Specifically, Dave would ask, "How many did Buster do on this one?" I would confer with the other instructor, tell Dave, and he would try to match Buster rep for rep (as Buster was older and stronger than Dave, the two of them performed the exercises at different resistances). This worked well to help keep both of them motivated and interested in the workouts.

- ***Instruct with simple but vivid words and phrases.*** While some of the teens I've worked with are quite precocious, instructing younger children can be a real challenge. How does one get a ten-year-old to sit with his head in the correct position and communicate effectively with his working musculature? I've found that taking extra time to show a younger child exactly what I want helps. Some children respond very well to visual methods of learning and thrive by mimicking my movements, so I'll demonstrate the exercise motion in front of them and have them follow me.

- ***Kids will tell you exactly what they want.*** Adults are often embarrassed to admit that they have exercise goals other than health and wellness. I suppose in getting past a certain age, "getting big biceps" as your primary goal for working out is frowned upon. Children and teens have no problem telling you exactly what they want. They know exactly what they want from the training, which is every-thing from "I want to climb up the rope in gym class" to "I want to make the varsity soccer team." One child I worked with had no exercise goals per se, but he had no illusions or misgivings about the training or his reasons for exercise ("I'm here because my mother thinks I need to work out").

- ***Encouragement and positive reinforcement.*** It's helpful to keep the weight training sessions positive and encouraging, so the child sees the workout as an opportunity to grow rather than an obstacle in their day. When instructing kids, I try to avoid the word "don't," lest they feel like I'm scold-ing them and become unresponsive. Instead, I'll tell them to do what it is I want them to do, instead of what I don't want them to do. I've found that telling a younger trainee to "straighten your wrists" works far better than "don't bend your wrists."

- ***Willingness to adapt the exercises to the individual.***
  One of my initial concerns about training youngsters was
  realized when I worked with six-year-old Sarah who was
  so small she needed several additional seat pads as a
  makeshift booster seat and was too weak to even budge
  the handles on our Nautilus Overhead Press, even with the
  machine set to its lightest resistance. Rather than abandon
  this exercise and its potential benefits, we decided to adapt
  the exercise to her by employing rep assists—a technique
  where the instructor assists in lifting the weight, then allows
  the child to lower the full weight by herself. (Muscles are
  stronger when lowering weight than when lifting weight.)
  Using this technique, Sarah was able to build strength
  over time, eventually reaching the ability to lift and lower
  the weight without assistance for several repetitions.

I'm convinced that strength training is a safe and productive
method for trainees of all ages. Children and young adults
can and should be encouraged to partake in regular strength
training for their health and well-being. The experiences I've
had training children, adolescents, and young adults lead me
to believe that they should be treated with the same care,
attention, and respect as adults.

And I guarantee that, as a parent or caregiver, you will feel
just as Mr. Thong does once you and your child start the slow
speed training program.

?

DID YOU KNOW? There are 10 teaspoons of sugar in a
12-ounce can of soda—20 times more sugar than the normal
amount for your child's blood?

THE SLOW SPEED GYM ROUTINE

"A carpenter is only as good as his tools."
—ANONYMOUS

A home program is a great way to make you or your child stronger, but if you can join a gym or health club, the results will be superior. And the reason is that the equipment that most gyms have are likely to be superior to a home workout setup.

I suggest using machines when training in the gym because free weights (barbells and dumbbells) are more complicated to set up, awkward to learn, and more dangerous to use. Free weights can be used quite productively under good supervision but will not produce better benefits than machines. Many well-meaning coaches promote the use of free weights and claim that they are better for developing size, strength, and coordination. But there is not a shred of scientific evidence to support this claim. In fact, there are a few exercises that can only be performed on a good machine. In other words, there is nothing that free weights can provide that machines can't—but not vice versa!

When you search for gyms in your area, check to see if they have child-size exercise machines. More and more gyms are starting to include these devices in their clubs. Once a child is over 5 feet tall, most adult-size machines will work just fine. But sometimes not. So it is always a good idea to seek the help of a qualified trainer in the gym to help set your child up on the machines in the proper manner, meaning, the correct setting for the seats, hand placement, and so forth. A lot of machines have instructional stickers that tell you how to set a person in the machine and how to use them. Sometimes they are good, sometimes they're not, so ask a trainer or manager how to set you and your child up in the machines properly.

I find that Serious Strength has given me and my son enduring strength, literally. The pace and the precision of the whole program is what I would call a program of strength development for life. This means, you're in it for the long haul, hopefully for the rest of your life. The slow movement and focus of the program creates not only a strong body but also a strong mind/body awareness. It has helped him to keep injuries from occurring on the field. In short, we both love it and are in it for the long haul!

—**Lynette and Byron J.**

Choosing the Right Weight

Setting the proper amount of weight for each exercise is a bit tricky. If you're unfamiliar with using machines, again seek the help of a qualified trainer in the gym. But if you are familiar with the weight machines, determine the right amount of weight for your child by allowing for at least 60 seconds worth of work (5 repetitions) before muscular success and not more than 90 seconds (9 repetitions). Many machines have weight stacks that are numbered in a completely arbitrary fashion—totally random in most cases. Although you might think that these numbers correlate directly to an exact number in pounds or kilograms you are lifting, the truth is that they usually don't. What I mean is that even though the weights themselves weigh what the sticker says, the distance they travel upward matters to how heavy they feel. Sometimes a 50-pound starting weight will feel heavy on one brand of machine while it will feel light on the same machine made by another company because the other company's machine was designed with a shorter distance for the weight to travel when the weight is lifted. So, you'll need to use trial and error to get the right weight for each exercise.

Start with the lightest weights on the machines and see if it is easy for the child to do. Usually, most machines have very light starting weights. If the starting weight is too heavy, then you'll have to skip that exercise on that particular machine. But this should be rare. If you wish, you can assist the child in the lifting portion, being careful to control the weight to the top and allow the child to lower the weight back down on her own. You have to make sure that the transfer of the weight is done slowly and gradually so that you do not just let go of the weight before the child has control of it.

For the child beginning a strength training program, the weight selected should feel relatively easy on the first repetition. It's important to remind the child not to start quickly even with a light weight, but to start each repetition very slowly as if sneaking up behind someone.

As the child becomes familiar with the machines little by little you should add resistance (weight), endeavoring to reach the greatest level of fatigue between 5 and 9 repetitions. If he can continue to lift and lower the weight smoothly and in perfect slow form for at least 60 seconds, the weight is not too heavy. If he honestly can't make the 60-second mark (5 repetitions) before reaching muscular success, the weight is a little too heavy. Lower the weight a bit for him on the next session. If, on the other hand, he's still moving along in the exercise like the Energizer Bunny, the weight is too light and you'll want to increase it by a notch at the next session. Of course, when you've found the right weights, write them down on the workout progress chart.

Upping the Ante

Instead of waiting until your child can continue to lift beyond 9 reps or longer than 90 seconds, increase the weight for a particular machine in small increments—even as little as 1 or 2 pounds—when you begin to see progress moving toward those maximums. For example, on week one you begin an exercise with your child using 50 pounds. It takes him 4 repetitions to reach muscular success. The next weekly session you do the exercise again and your child does 7 repetitions. The next week you do the exercise again and he gets 8 repetitions. But subsequent sessions find him only able to achieve the 8 repetitions. He just can't seem to get to 9. If you see this happening after a few sessions, raise the weight up a tiny bit anyway. Even a half pound is fine. This way, you'll stay in the scientific time zone during every exercise. By making these small incremental increases—a technique I call micro-loading—your child (and you) can make steady and amazing increases in strength.

In a well equipped gym, the machines will have add-on weights, also known as saddle plates, that fit on the main weight stacks allowing you to make smaller and more precise adjustments. These additional weights may come in increments as small as 1/4 pound. But many gyms may only have 5 or 10 pound add-on saddle plates. If possible, nudge your gym manager into purchasing a few inexpensive add-on plates for the gym so that you and your child (and everyone else for that matter) can benefit. (See the Appendix for equipment resources.)

There are dozens of different exercises that a child can do. To keep it simple and uncomplicated, I've listed ten exercises that will address every major muscle group either directly or indirectly. For example, if you do a biceps (upper arm) curl, you work the biceps muscles *directly* and the muscles of the forearm *indirectly.* When you do leg curls, you work the hamstrings *directly* and the calf muscles *indirectly.* So if your child performs all of the exercises listed, it will be an extremely comprehensive total body workout.

The ten exercises are as follows:

1. Chest press or bench press

2. Pull-downs or lat pulls

3. Overhead press or military shoulder press

4. Rowing back or rear deltoid

5. Biceps curls or arm curls

6. Leg press or squats

7. Hamstring curls or leg curls

8. Hip adduction or inner thigh

9. Abdominal flexion or ab crunches

10. Lumbar extension or lower back

Doing ten exercises in one fell swoop asks a lot of some younger kids' attention spans and their concentration will probably wane toward the end of the program. I recommend that you select six or seven of the exercises—depending on the availability of machines in your gym—and perform them *in the exact order given.* As your child gets the hang of them, you can add a few more, building to a total of eight or nine or all ten. Many gyms do not have a Lower Back Machine. But that's okay because this machine is not as important for kids as it is for adults.

The exercises to focus on are highlighted and include:

- Hamstring curl

- Leg press

- Chest press

- Pull-down

- Shoulder press

These five are the most important exercises and should always be performed at each session.

FREQUENCY OF WORKOUTS

As with the home program, I recommend two weekly workouts. My opinion and research on the subject indicate pretty strongly that two workout sessions per week are better than one. One session provides good but not optimal benefits. The one caveat is if your child is a very active athlete. If so, one session seems to work as well as two mainly because more recovery time is needed to allow for the positive adaptations to occur. Athletic kids are usually playing and practicing almost every day. Therefore, their bodies are in a constant state of breakdown. Strength training is also an activity that breaks down the body in order to build it up. Therefore, recovery is limited in the athlete and recovery is necessary for strength to occur.

But either way, consistency is the key ingredient, so try to get in at least one session per week. Some people prefer to do two very short sessions per week. It's up to you to decide. But know that kids tend to get bored with something they do too often, so I don't suggest doing more than two sessions a week.

Here are the basic rules of thumb for exercising on machines:

- Complete all repetitions in as perfect form as possible. Avoid straining, twisting, excessive sudden arching of the back, craning the neck, slouching, or jerking the weight to complete a repetition. Don't bang, drop, or slam the weights.

- Remind yourself and your child that the real objective is to reach muscular success—the deepest level of fatigue in the target muscle(s)—not to complete a certain number of repetitions in any way possible.

- Always breathe in a relaxed, even fashion throughout the exercise and allow for continued breathing as the exercises get more challenging. Tell your child to "Breathe like a steam engine!" or "Pretend that you are Superman huffing and puffing a hurricane away!"

- Try to keep a neutral, focused, and concentrated attitude during the exercise. Try to limit teeth clenching and grimacing because it makes it easier to hold the breath. Remember to say: "Make a face like you're seeing a ghost!"

- Always work through a full, pain-free range of joint motion.

- Remember the timing: Take 5 counts to lift the weight in a smooth, slow fashion, moving the weight at a pace of about 1 inch per second (a minimum of 5 beats of the metronome to complete the lift); make a very slow reversal of direction, taking 1 or 2 beats to complete the change; reverse direction and finish the repetition just as slowly, moving the weight about 1 inch a second on its return to the starting position.

Because your child's safety must always come first, along with this list of exercises for a Slow Burn workout in the gym, you'll find some important do's and don'ts that are specific to each one. Take them to heart.

I've given each of the exercises a couple of different names that are usually what the exercise is called. If for some reason the machines you use have different names than the ones I've used, ask a qualified trainer or the manager of the gym to help you out and make sure you are using the correct devices.

MACHINE EXERCISES

CHEST PRESS OR BENCH PRESS

This exercise works the muscles of the chest (pectorals), as well as the muscles of the arms (triceps) and shoulders (front deltoids).

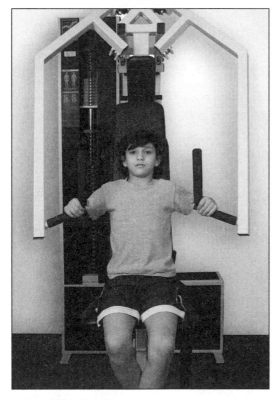

Start/Finish Position

Halfway/Endpoint

TELL YOUR CHILD

- **DO** keep your shoulders down.

- **DO** keep your chin slightly tucked and your neck elongated.

- **DO** keep your chest "proud" and upright.

- **DO** keep your elbows at 45-degrees from your sides.

- **DO** keep a slight bend in your elbows at the finish point.

- **DO** keep your hands in line with your armpits at the start.

- **DO** keep your lower back slightly arched throughout.

- **DO** keep your hands loose around the grip(s).

- **DON'T** shrug your shoulders.

- **DON'T** crane your neck or tip your head back and chin up.

- **DON'T** slouch or let your chest "cave in."

- **DON'T** lock your elbows at the finish point.

- **DON'T** let your hands and arms rise above the level of your shoulders or drop below your rib cage.

- **DON'T** arch suddenly to finish a repetition.

- **DON'T** tightly grip the handles or bar.

HIP ABDUCTION OR INNER THIGH

This exercise works the inner thighs and the hip muscles (hip adductors or the horseback riding muscles).

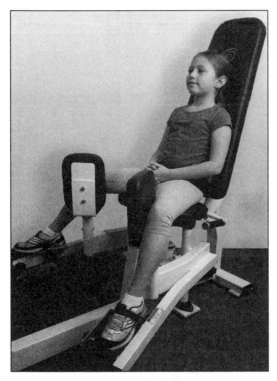

Start/Finish Position

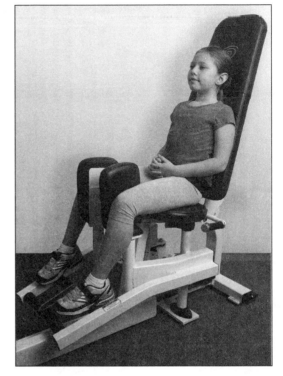

Halfway/Endpoint

TELL YOUR CHILD

- **DO** keep your thighs straight and your kneecaps and toes pointed toward the ceiling.

- **DON'T** let your thighs, knees, and toes rotate outward.

LEG PRESS, LEG SLED, OR SQUAT

This exercise works the buttocks (gluteus) and muscles of both the front and back of the thighs (quadriceps and hamstrings).

Start/Finish Position

Halfway/Endpoint

TELL YOUR CHILD

- **DO** keep your knees slightly bent at the endpoint.

- **DO** keep your hands loosely gripped on the handles (if any) or off the handles completely and relaxed at your sides.

- **DO** keep your legs parallel to each other, your knees and toes aligned, and your feet spaced a hip's width apart.

- **DON'T** lock your knees.

- **DON'T** grip the handles tightly or put your hands on your thighs to push.

- **DON'T** let your knees knock together or your feet turn out.

KNEE FLEXION OR LEG CURL

Works the muscles of the back of the thighs (hamstrings) and the calves

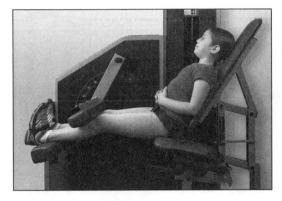

Start/Finish Position

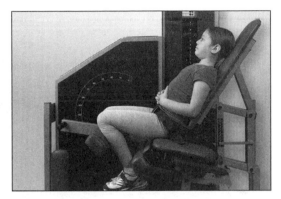

Halfway/Endpoint

TELL YOUR CHILD

- **DO** align your knee joint with the axis of rotation of the machine (ask an onsite expert to check).

- **DO** keep your kneecaps facing the ceiling and your legs parallel.

- **DO** keep your toes flexed toward you as if they were reaching for your knees.

- **DO** let your back arch naturally.

- **DON'T** attempt the exercise with your knee joint in front of or behind the axis of rotation of the machine.

- **DON'T** spread your ankles apart.

- **DON'T** point your toes.

- **DON'T** suddenly arch your back.

SHOULDER SIDE RAISES OR LATERAL RAISE

This exercise works the shoulders (including the deltoids).

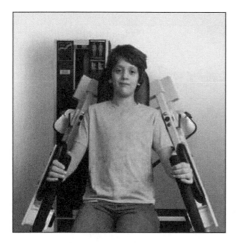

Start/Finish Position

Halfway/Endpoint

TELL YOUR CHILD

- **DO** keep your back snugly against the back pad.

- **DO** pause at the point that your arms are parallel to the ground or slightly above parallel.

- **DON'T** lean forward or arch your back excessively.

- **DON'T** raise your elbows and arms above shoulder height.

OVERHEAD SHOULDER PRESS OR MILITARY PRESS

This exercise works the shoulders (deltoids) and the muscles on the backs of the arms (triceps).

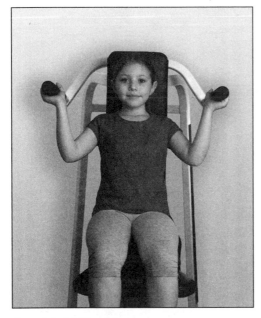

Start/Finish Position

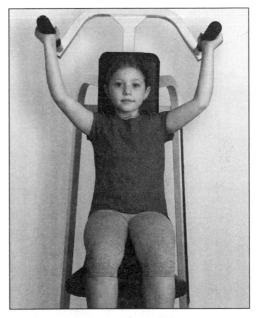

Halfway/Endpoint

TELL YOUR CHILD

- **DO** keep your hands slightly in front of your shoulders.

- **DO** keep your back flat (against the back pad if there is one) with good upright posture and a "proud" chest.

- **DON'T** position your hands beside or behind your shoulders.

- **DON'T** slouch down or "cave" your chest.

- **DON'T** violently arch your back.

- **DON'T** grip your hands too tightly.

ROWING BACK OR ROW TORSO

This exercise works the muscles of the upper back and shoulders (trapezius, rhomboids, rear deltoids).

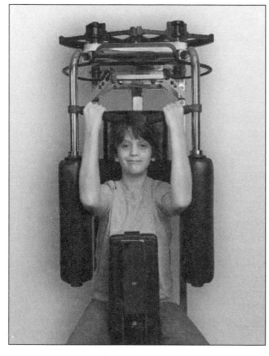

Start/Finish Position

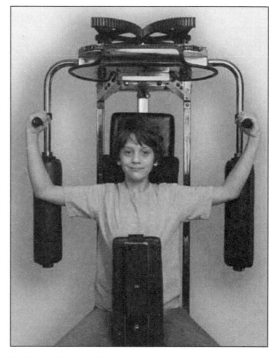

Halfway/Endpoint

TELL YOUR CHILD

- **DO** sit up tall, keeping your shoulders down.

- **DO** press the pads away using your forearms and elbows.

- **DO** keep your arms parallel to the ground.

- **DON'T** shrug your shoulders.

- **DON'T** lurch backward.

- **DON'T** raise or lower your elbows from a parallel position.

BACK PULL-DOWNS OR LAT PULL-DOWNS

This exercise works the muscles of the back ("lats"), the muscles of the front of the arms (biceps and triceps), and the muscles of the forearms.

Start/Finish Position   **Halfway/Endpoint**

TELL YOUR CHILD

- **DO** use a "palms-facing-you" grip (A palms-facing-away grip twists the forearm and makes the biceps weaker, thus shortchanging the benefit of the exercise).

- **DO** place your hands a shoulder's width apart.

- **DO** keep a slight bend in the elbows when starting.

- **DON'T** position your hands too close together or too wide apart.

- **DON'T** allow your elbows to "lock" straight in extension.

BICEPS CURL OR ARM CURL

This exercise works the muscles of the front of the upper arm (biceps) and the muscles of the forearm.

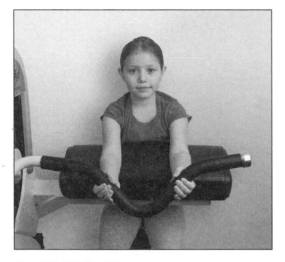

Start/Finish Position

Halfway/Endpoint

TELL YOUR CHILD

- **DO** keep your shoulders down.

- **DO** keep your elbows slightly bent at extension.

- **DON'T** shrug or hunch your shoulders.

- **DON'T** allow your elbows to fully straighten or "lock" at extension.

ABDOMINAL CRUNCHES OR AB CURL

This exercise works the "stomach" muscles or "abs."

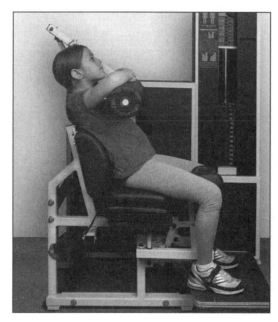

Start/Finish Position

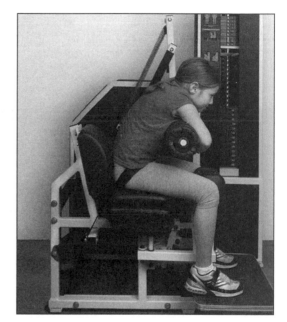

Halfway/Endpoint

TELL YOUR CHILD

- **DO** keep your head and neck straight and relaxed.

- **DO** flex your spine and curl your trunk.

- **DON'T** flex or extend your neck.

- **DON'T** pivot at your hips.

LOWER BACK OR BACK EXTENSION

This exercise works the muscles of the lower back (lumbar area).

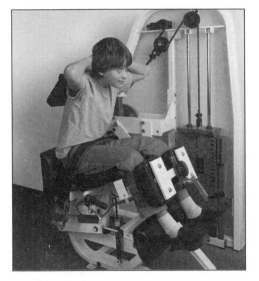

Start/Finish Position

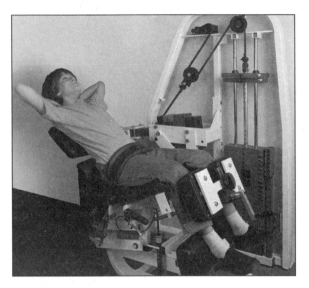

Halfway/Endpoint

TELL YOUR CHILD

- **DO** use the seat belt to keep your pelvis still if there is one.

- **DO** sit up tall and straight at the start.

- **DO** arch your back fully at the finish.

- **DON'T** allow yourself to pivot from your hips or you won't be working your back. You want to make sure that the fulcrum or pivot point is the lower back or lower spine.

- **DON'T** twist or shift side to side as you lean back.

- **DON'T** slouch in the finish.

PARENT TO PARENT

My son Ephraim is ten years old. He is an aspiring cartoonist; more artsy than sporty. He has an average build, and has asthma, eczema, food allergies, and environmental allergies. He has good coping skills, but he thinks all the health stuff is a drag.

Ephraim was eight years old when he began working with Fred. After taking measurements, and getting whatever history and medical information necessary, Ephraim went to the equipment to start learning the exercises. As I knew the level of intensity at Serious Strength from my own weight training, I was a bit anxious about Ephraim's ability to handle a challenging workout. They, of course, started him light and easy and almost two years later, he is using weights that amaze me. Remember, he is not a soccer kid, he's an artist/video gamer. Okay, that is the history. What has it done for Ephraim?

He has developed strength and confidence and a great amount of self-esteem. His tennis coach has remarked on several occasions how much harder and stronger he is hitting the ball. Because he has a compromised respiratory situation, it is important to help him be as strong as he can be. He comes out of his training session adding and multiplying in his head the amount of weight he lifted. He is wiped out, but recovers pretty quickly. As his mom, I know this training is incredibly challenging for my son. I know having Ephraim challenge himself physically like this is a fantastic hurdle for him. I see him growing from a pretty scrawny-looking kid to a confident ten-year-old, who is getting stronger, and whose tennis grip is now pretty awesome. This has been a totally positive experience for him.

—**Connie S.**

POST WORKOUT CHOW

After each workout, the child should have a good meal rich in healthy fats and proteins. For example, you can make your child a rollup using fresh roast beef, turkey, ham, or whatever is the favorite meat of choice. You can add some cheese, a tablespoon of almond butter (if your child tolerates nuts), and an apple, some berries, or half a banana.

It appears from much scientific (as well as anecdotal) evidence that it is best to eat a post-exercise meal within an hour of the child's (or your) workout session. Why? It is when the body is most ready to absorb all of the nutrients and to begin the rebuilding process to build more bone, muscle, strength, and endurance. So pump up and then chow down.

C H A P T E R

The Strong Kids,
Healthy Kids Eating Plan*

"You are what you eat."
—ANONYMOUS

Let's face it, kids like to eat what they like to eat. And often what they like to eat is not what we'd like them to eat. This is often because we eat what we don't want them to eat and so they want to eat it, too. Yes—if you want your kids to eat right, you've got to eat right as well. But what is "eating right"?

* Note: It is well beyond the scope of this book to address food allergies and other food-related health issues specific to your child. The following plan assumes that your child is free from any major food allergy, diseases, or illnesses.

If you've already been successful at getting your child or children to eat their eggs, meat (this includes fish and poultry), and veggies, great job! (Getting kids to eat fruit is generally not a problem.) These are the most important foods for your kids to eat because they contain all of the vital nutrients they need—every single last one of them.

If this is the case and you want to boost your kids' physical as well as mental health up a notch, while becoming or staying strong and fit, here's what to do. Remove or limit the amount of starches and grain sugars like potatoes, wheat, rice, and oats—all grain products for that matter. There is abundant evidence that grain products possess proteins and antinutrients that are known to be harmful to humans. I'll talk more about this problem a bit later in this section.

I won't mention trying to limit their intake of sugary sodas, candy, cookies, and all commercially made snacks. I think by now we all know that these sugary demons should be kept to a minimum, only for occasional consumption. And of course there are natural sugars and unnatural (high fructose corn syrup) sugars that should always be avoided. Still, try and keep these to a minimum.

The plan I propose is not a diet. Instead, it is a real food plan that allows for dozens of healthy food choices that kids love and never make them feel restricted or deprived. In short, diets screw us all up, especially kids. So what do I mean by "real food"? According to my friend Nina Planck in her book, *Real Food: What to Eat and Why,* real food is food that is not commercially created. A real food is an apple, a carrot, chicken, fish, anything that grows, swims, walks, or flies.

According to Planck:

> Real food is anything you'd find around the perimeter of the supermarket, rather than in the center. That means fresh beef, pork, poultry, and fish; all the simple dairy foods—milk, yogurt, cheese, butter—but not the processed stuff with lots of ingredients; eggs; all the nuts, seeds, fruits, and vegetables. Add to that other traditional, old-fashioned fats with a history

(like olive oil and coconut oil) and you'll be in good shape. Don't eat the packaged foods from the center aisles. Industrial food is the opposite of real food. Industrial food is new and it's full of new ingredients (margarine made with corn oil, or soy bean juice with added DHA from algae). Real food is old and it has the same ingredients it always had: wild salmon, butter, almonds, and whole eggs. The recipe for yogurt—whole milk and cultures—hasn't changed in 4,500 years. Why should it? The surprising thing about child nutrition is just how vital the real foods are. Once we grow up, we can probably get away with big salads with some chicken on top. And we need lots of fresh fruits and vegetables. But from birth to two years, and indeed right through the teen years, the overwhelming needs are for high-quality fat and protein to promote growth and development. As we grow up, we need to eat more fruits and vegetables for potassium, vitamin C, antioxidants, and fiber. But for little humans, the more good fats and good protein, the better. Oddly enough, cereal is definitely not the ideal food for young babies or children. They need meat and egg yolks much more than grains. In fact, grains are not needed at all as all of the nutrients that grains provide are present in the aforementioned foods.

All of the foods I list in the separate categories can be eaten by you or your child to your heart's content. No calorie counting is necessary. Counting calories, as most dieticians recommend doing, rarely works for the long haul. And these foods are very satiating because they are so high in essential nutrients.

DID YOU KNOW? *Meat, eggs, and dairy are the only foods that contain vitamin B12, which is necessary for the synthesis of red blood cells, the maintenance of the nervous system, and growth and development in children?*

Whether your goal is to get your child to eat better for reasons of general health, fat loss, sports performance, or all three, eating healthfully will do the trick.

The most important aspect of the feeding frenzy is education, especially if you've not been successful in getting your child to eat right. Kids love to learn. And when we teach them the truth about the foods we want them to eat, rather than saying, "Eat this 'cuz I said so!" they appreciate the lesson, they feel your caring, and then they make the smart choice more easily and more readily. And let's face it, when they can get their hands on the junk they will. But it is my experience that when their hands are on the junk, and they know it is junk, they will consider it more readily and often eat or drink less of it.

For example, my wife and I spend a few minutes at most meals saying things like "Broccoli is for bones!" and "Meat is for muscles." If my six-year-old daughter, Amber (who is a pasta freak), refuses to eat her meat for some reason one can't possibly fathom—since she gobbled all her meat up the night before—I gently squeeze her upper arm and say, "Hmm… feels like your muscles are getting softer, Ambie—I dunno." Almost always after saying something like this, she pops down a few squares of steak and says, "Feel it now, Dad!"

A SUGAR STORY

As we all know, sugar is perhaps the biggest problem facing parents and caregivers in the nutritional fight for children's health. Fact: A single can of cola has 39 grams of sugar, or about 10 teaspoons. This is 20 times more sugar than the normal amount in the bloodstream of a child. At a water park one summer day, my daughters and I sat to have some lunch after hours of fun and frolic. My daughter asked me, "Dad, can I have a soda?" I said, "Sure, love, but remember what soda does to your blood." Georgia replied, "It makes your blood

Our kids (Becca, age 8, and Adam, age 12) feel stronger and are proud of their accomplishments since starting Slow Burn strength training and eating more healthfully as Fred suggests. We are doing something very healthy as a family and, in the process, teaching our children how important it is to take care of their bodies.

—Joyce and Jay H.

unhappy." "Righto," I said and left it at that. No lecture. No finger wagging. Sure enough she drank less than half of it. I know this story sounds a little too *Leave It to Beaver*-ish, but it's true. As I sit here and write this for you, I'm listening to my daughters tell their mother who is preparing their lunch, "Mom, I'll have some pasta with my hamburger, but not too much." I kid you not. (As you'll discover soon, pasta is not exactly a good source of anything and is one of the foods that contribute to obesity.)

Full disclosure of the foods and their benefits seems to work like a charm. Teach their brains rather than twist their arms and you'll be surprised how responsive they will be to eating what's good for them. In this way, it empowers them for making the right choices as they grow into teens or, if teens already, as they mature into adulthood. The following information will get you started on becoming knowledgeable about the different foods that are good, bad, and really ugly.

Freedom from the Junk

The nice thing about this approach is that you'll naturally stop buying the junk. The sweetest thing you'll ever hear is when you offer chips or cookies to your child and she responds by saying, "Sure dad, but are there any more of those strawberries?" Sigh.

Let's face it, the food companies are never ever going to stop making the endless amounts of crud they push like breakfast cereals and soft drinks. Never, that is, until we stop buying them. We forced cigarette companies to place warnings on their labels, but we don't require similar warnings from manufacturers of chemicals, fake sweeteners, and appetite-enhancing substances that are known to damage our children's health. We even make laws governing the age for smoking and drinking alcohol, but for drinking soda pop? No way.

HEALTH TIP: *Sound sleep is when the body recharges so make sure your child gets enough. Early to bed really does make a kid healthy and wise.*

PLENTY OF PROTEIN

Proteins are the building materials that the human body needs to survive, regenerate tissues, especially muscle tissue, and perform numerous other complicated and life-giving tasks. The word *protein* comes from the Greek word *prota,* meaning "of primary importance." Protein is indeed of primary importance not only for adults but especially for growing boys and girls. And they need plenty of it. Without adequate protein in the diet, a child will not realize his or her full physical potential.

The types of proteins matter, and they matter a lot. Only meats provide all of the essential amino acids that the body needs for maintaining a healthy self. Although plants and grains contain many proteins, none provide all of the essential amino acids. If we only ate plants, grains, and fruits our health would eventually suffer unless we took a boatload of expensive supplements. This is why some vegetarians and all vegans need to take supplements to stay healthy. This is not said to denigrate the lifestyle choice of people who choose not to eat animals. Not at all. It is simply a fact that should be understood—and respected.

HEALTH TIP: *Boil or poach your eggs instead of scrambling. It keeps the fat in the yolk from being damaged.*

Red meats are a great source of protein. I know this statement is contrary to a lot of nutritional advice you might read today about limiting protein and avoiding red meat, but there is no scientific evidence to support the claim that red meat in and of itself is a danger. I maintain that kids who are growing and working to increase muscle mass need quality protein. The best protein available is from meat that comes from organically fed, free-range animals. If your child is a vegetarian, you have to do some extra work to make sure that your child gets the protein he or she needs to build strong muscles. I encourage you to consult a nutritionist or your pediatrician to make sure that you're getting enough protein and essential vitamins and minerals for your child to reach his or her growth potential.

Grass-Fed Meats

Grass-fed animals are a healthier choice than primarily grain-fed animals. Grass is the natural food for most meat-producing animals and it stands to reason that the healthier the animal you eat, the healthier you will be, too. In the Appendix, I've listed a great resource for purchasing meat from grass-fed animals and for learning about why the choice is a plus for you and your child's body. I urge you to take the time and learn all you can about this.

The Price of Food

Many people worry that healthier food—organic, less processed, natural food—can be more expensive when you go to the store. But you will find that making healthier choices saves you money. Processed foods, frozen foods, and sugary snacks tend to be more expensive than produce, meats, and dairy products. If you buy real food, you will find your grocery budget goes farther and gets your family more nutrition and more filling meals for the same money you could spend on all those things you aren't supposed to buy.

Other common misconceptions are that eating too much protein prevents the body from absorbing certain vitamins and minerals, which in turn affects the immune system, and that it can weaken bones and cause osteoporosis. Although it is true that if you eat huge amounts of protein, your body will use some bone calcium to buffer the acid created by the protein, grains are much worse on this score. You need only eat a little bit of fruit, and vegetables to spare your bone mass. In short, far from fearing protein, you should make sure to include it as roughly 30 percent to 40 percent of your child's diet. And remember: don't trim too much of the fat.

Feel free to eat any and all protein to your heart's content at any meal and at any time. Contrary to what you hear on TV or in the news, you do not need to eat lean proteins. In fact, if there is too little fat in the diet, your body will not be able to process the proteins you eat as effectively nor will your body be able to absorb and use the vitamins and minerals from your foods nearly as well. (See pages 102–103 for more information on what types of fats are part of a healthy diet.)

I suggest the following protein sources:

- Eggs (poached, soft boiled, overeasy are best so as not to cook the yolk, which damages its fat content)

- Cheese

- Fish

- Protein shakes (the purest, non-denatured protein products come from a company called Well Wisdom)

- Cottage cheese

- Bacon, sausage, and ham steaks (but sugar-free, so read those labels! It is also best to refrain from nitrates. Always try and choose sausages made from organic and grass fed animals)

- Hamburger

- Roast beef

- Steak

- Chicken

- Turkey

- Pork

- Veal

- Fish (tuna, salmon, and sardines)

- Shellfish (allergies aside)

- Tuna, chicken, and egg salads

Eating enough protein is very important. Without enough protein, your body will quite literally eat up its own muscle tissue to make up for the shortfall. So I've created a cheat sheet to help you out. Make sure that at each meal (breakfast, lunch, and dinner) your child is getting several ounces of high-quality protein from the sources listed below. With this protein serving, along with some veggies and fruit, you're on the money. This will ensure that your child will have the building blocks needed to support this strength training program.

The list below contains the grams and calories for each of the foods. Don't fret over or even think about the calories. What matters is that at every main meal (as often as possible), you're providing protein to your child.

PROTEIN SOURCES (Most serving sizes are 1 cup = 8 oz)

Chicken	1 cup: chopped, meat only—40.5g/266 cal
	1/2 chicken w/skin, roasted—81.6g/715 cal
Beef	4 oz: hamburger, cooked—27g/328 cal
Fish	1 cup: solid white tuna in water—60g/280 cal
	4 oz: salmon, baked—25g/234 cal
Tofu	1 cup: fresh—20g/188 cal
	1 cup: firm—40g/366 cal
Beans	1 cup: baked—12g/300 cal
	1 cup: black—12g/200 cal
	1 cup: green soybeans, boiled—22g/254 cal
Nuts	1 cup: cashews—24g/800 cal
	1 cup: almonds—24g/720 cal
	1 cup: peanuts—44g/1080 cal
	1 cup: walnuts—15g/660 cal
Dairy	1 cup: cheddar cheese—28g/480 cal
	1 cup: cottage cheese 4% fat/14g, 120 cal
	1 cup: plain yogurt—12g/150 cal
	1 cup: whole cow's milk—8g, 150 cal
	1 cup: skim cow's milk—8g, 80 cal
	1 cup: soy milk—8g/140 cal
Eggs	1 whole egg—6.3g/75 cal
	1 cup: chopped, hardboiled—17g/210 cal
Pork	1 cup: ham, 11% fat, chopped—31.7g/249 cal
	Bacon, 2 slices—5g/80 cal
	Sausage, 2 links—9g/180 cal

A Word on Dairy Products

Dairy products, including all kinds of cheese, yogurt, whole milk, and whole cream, are a good source of protein and calcium. They do, however, contain a lot of sugars, so try not to let your child gorge on milk or other high sugar dairy items. There seems to be abundant evidence that organic products contain more of the nutrients you need and tend to be less processed. It is true that organic dairy products are pricier, but if you can work them into your food budget, they are worth the added expense. Finding local farmers and food co-ops can also be a good way of getting organic and less-processed products more economically.

HIGH-QUALITY FATS AND OILS

Research indicates that a much larger percentage of the essential micronutrients are absorbed by the body when the diet is high in fat. The quality of the fat is of great importance. Good fats are used to rebuild your body and will help to maintain a proper hormone level, leading to better sleep, concentration, and better skin, hair, and nails, as well as slowing down the aging process.

HEALTH TIP: *Eating healthy fats (e.g., olive oil, avocados) with your vegetables dramatically improves the absorption of the vitamins and minerals within them.*

Saturated fats get a really bad rap and are far from the demons a lot of health organizations claim them to be. These are the fats found in eggs, red meat, and tropical oils like coconut oil. The reason for this bad rap is that many of these organizations lump all fats together, never differentiating between the good fats and the bad fats, and thus draw incorrect conclusions. This is a shame because these good fats are critical for establishing a healthy hormonal tone for you and your child. Fat, if it's a real fat, one that occurs in nature like egg yolks, coconut, avocados, and so on, should be a major part of your and your child's diet.

Try your best to avoid all partially hydrogenated vegetable oils, which are the bad fats. And they are bad because they are unnatural and damaged, which leads to damage within the cells of your body. Try not to use too much of the following oils:

- Corn oil

- Safflower oil

- Soybean oil

- Sunflower oil

- Canola oil

- Vegetable shortenings

- Vegetable cooking oils

In *The Protein Power Lifeplan,* Drs. Michael and MaryDan Eades explain that good fats, which are not processed and are eaten largely as they are found in nature, are necessary for a healthy diet.

The good fats and oils are:

- Butter (cook with low heat as it can burn and become damaged)

- Ghee (clarified butter—all the sugar is removed)

- Olive oil (not for deep frying)

- Nut and fruit oils (almond, avocado, sesame, walnut, and the like)

- Coconut oil (best for deep frying)

- Cream

- Bird fat (chicken, turkey, etc.)

- Lard

There are many more, but these are a good start and offer a wide range of choices.

FEWER SUGARS AND CARBS

Grains possess a host of what are called antinutrients, which are best left out of your body.

Grains, in all their forms, are carbohydrates (sugars). Most people easily recognize that cakes, cookies, and pies are sugar and should be eaten sparingly. But these same folks think that a bowl of hearty oatmeal is really healthy. Well let's change that thought process. Just like cake and candy, all carbohydrates including that hearty oatmeal and brown rice are sugar. So the same way you don't eat cake all day, think of all grain-based carbohydrates as a special treat to be eaten occasionally and only in small quantities.

This applies to all kinds of carbohydrates, including pasta, bagels, cereals, bread, rice, wheat, oats, cookies, cakes, sodas, candy, chips, grain flours, pretzels, Pop-tarts, and a thousand other foods along these lines.

Does this mean your child can never, ever again have pizza or a peanut-butter-and-jelly sandwich? No, of course not. Just work hard to minimize these empty calories, and your child will be as fit as a fiddle in no time.

Kids today (and adults for that matter) who are overfat are that way because they eat too much carbohydrate (sugar). If every single person decreased the carbohydrate content in their diets to no more than 100 grams daily, there would be an enormous decline in obesity (not to mention a decline in adult-onset diabetes, and many other symptoms associated with high blood sugar levels). It is really this simple. Let me explain.

Insulin is the primary metabolic hormone responsible for both storing fat in the fat cells and, more important, keeping it there. If your insulin levels are too high, fat is on a direct, non-stop route into the fat cell. It's pretty much trapped there until insulin levels fall, allowing fat to escape.

When you go on a low-sugar diet, you reduce insulin levels dramatically, and it happens pretty quickly. You put yourself into a metabolic situation in which fat can easily flow from the fat cell to the tissues where it is burned. Think of it as being stuck in a jail cell. When you eat too much sugar, be it in the form of whole-grain bread, pasta, oatmeal, pie, or cake, you create an efficient transportation system to get the fat prisoner to fat cell prison and open up the jail cell for holding the fat prisoner. Once the fat is in, the cell door slams shut and, as long as you keep eating a lot of sugar, the fat remains imprisoned.

When you reduce the amount of sugar in the diet, it is as if all of the prison guards have been bought off and the jail cell is left unlocked. The fat prisoners are free to flee. And flee they will if you keep up the good work.

So consider how you can improve on a simple breakfast. A single serving of toasted oat cereal has a whopping 27 grams of sugar. That's right, 27 grams! Now add a 1/2 cup of skim milk (6 grams), a slice of whole-wheat toast (20 grams), a tablespoon of jelly (15 grams), and an 8-ounce glass of orange juice (23.6 grams). Now add this up and what do we get?

We get 91.6 grams of sugar (and this is just for breakfast!), 348.5 calories, and 6 grams of fiber.

By contrast, let's look at the sugar content of a breakfast consisting of ham, eggs, yogurt, and berries (all organic, of course, when possible and if your budget allows).

This breakfast is one boiled or scrambled egg (0.6 grams), 4 ounces of full-fat plain yogurt (5.3 grams), 3 ounces fresh ham (0 grams); 25 little blueberries (5 grams), and a 1/2 cup of regular-size strawberries (6.35 grams). Add this up and what do we get?

We get 17.2 grams of sugar, 344.5 calories, and 2.45 grams of fiber.

Not only does this breakfast meal have dramatically less sugar, it contains far more healthy protein and fats for your growing child.

For a child looking to lose fat, once they begin eating a low-sugar diet, their fat will easily flow out of storage from the fat cells. Eating like this creates a natural and healthful caloric deficit compared to how the child ate before. When this happens, the additional calories required to run the child's growing body will come from the fat cells, which is exactly what you want to happen.

HEALTH TIP: *Microwaving destroys most of the vital nutrients in your food.*

Children of the Corn Syrup

Corn syrup, which is a fructose—in other words, a sugar—is among the worst sugars you can possibly eat. High-fructose corn syrup is even worse. It's a neurological *Nightmare on Health Street.* For quite some time, fructose (found in fruit, although only about 40 percent of fruit is fructose) was thought to be good for people who had diabetes and who wanted to lose weight because it's absorbed by the body a lot more rapidly than glucose and causes a smaller rise in blood sugar. However, there is a big difference in how these two common sugars are absorbed.

Research on specific hormonal factors suggests that fructose actually *promotes* disease more readily than glucose. Glucose is metabolized in every cell in the body, but all fructose must be metabolized inside your liver. And when the liver is asked to deal with a lot of sugar it can and does lead to fatty deposits and cirrhosis as seen in alcoholics. Fructose also draws a host of beneficial micronutrients needed to absorb it so that these micronutrients, rather than nourishing the body, are essentially wasted. To make matters worse, there is some thought that high-fructose corn syrup might be the cause of elevated cholesterol levels. It has also been found to inhibit the action of white blood cells, which compromises immune system function. If you think about it, this could cause or contribute to colds, infections, and other inflammatory maladies seen today in many youngsters.

High-fructose corn syrup can be found in almost every single packaged food in your local grocery store. Read those labels. If it says "corn syrup" or, more important, "high-fructose corn syrup" on the label, do yourself and your family a huge metabolic mitzvah (a *mitzvah* is a good deed) and *do not buy it!*

The bottom line is that you should be feeding your child real food—that is, food that once walked, crawled, or grew out of the ground. There's no such thing as a pasta tree or a bagel bush. In short, try not to feed your child food that has been made by man. If it comes in a box, don't eat it.

Strong children thrive. I know of no better way for adults to develop strength and the habit and pleasure of exercise than at Serious Strength using Fred Hahn's Slow Burn method. It is a safe, effective way to build muscle for life without stressing and injuring joints and bones (which are common problems associated with traditional sports and gym training techniques).

Childhood strength paves the way to the mature enjoyment of an active lifestyle. I can think of no safer way to advance adolescent strength than by using Slow Burn strength training.

Serious Strength has successfully seen me through four major orthopedic operations and continues to support my difficult work life. Being strong has helped me in every way and Serious Strength Slow Burn training is an essential ingredient of my life. The method allows me to maintain activity levels I thought I would never enjoy again.

—**Lucy Perrotta, MD, (pediatrics, neonatology)**

FRUITS AND VEGETABLES

Eating vegetables and fruits—vital sources of vitamins, minerals, and fiber—with your protein sources is important. Preparing vegetables is one of the easiest things to do and my best recommendation is simply to steam them, drain, butter, and salt to taste. You can prepare almost any veggie like this and my kids love them this way. You preserve all of the goodies in the veggies by steaming them. The next best way is to boil them and then drain, butter, salt, and spice to taste. Most kids won't eat raw veggies as readily as steamed (my kids don't) but raw is fine as well. In the recipe section at the back of the book, you'll find some simple to prepare and excellent recipes that will help you get more vegetables into your kid.

But whether you steam, boil, roast, or serve them raw, the thing to do for your child is to try many different ways to get them to eat veggies in the most sugarless fashion possible. And don't microwave the poor little veggies or you'll kill them. Microwaving food is a surefire way to destroy 90 percent of what is alive and good in the food you feed to your kids. I strongly suggest you research the issue of microwaving food and read all you can on the subject. Fat (the good fat) boosts the absorption of the vitamins and minerals from vegetables so don't be too shy with the butter or olive oil!

As for fruits, serve your child the ripest fruits possible with no added sugar. Some freshly whipped cream on top is a plus and again helps the body absorb the nutrients that lie within the fruit. Instead of after-dinner desserts, serve fruit and your children will love it. Fruit may seem boring, but you can make it more fun for younger kids with little bowls with funny eyeballs, goofy pictures on the inside, big wacky straws to suck up the excess juice, and funky spoons and forks to stab and scoop.

But here's the real secret—the fruit has to be sweet. As sweet as candy. If you choose poor quality fruit, you will prove to your kids that fruit tastes like corrugated cardboard. So how do you ensure sweet fruit? The key is ripeness. My wife is a master at picking out fruits that are so ripe and sweet they'd embarrass a bag of M&M's. Try it!

Here's a recommended list of vegetables that are by no means the only ones you can serve. All are chock full of the good stuff and offering your child a wide array of choices is the best way to discover what they might enjoy.

- Artichokes
- Asparagus
- Beets
- Broccoli
- Brussels sprouts
- Cabbage (coleslaw)
- Carrots
- Cauliflower
- Celery
- Cucumber
- Eggplant
- Green beans

- Lettuces
- Mushrooms
- Peppers
- Spinach
- Squashes
- Turnips

Here is a variety of fruits for your child to try:

- Apples
- Avocado
- Bananas *(preferably small ones as large ones contain a lot of sugar)*
- Berries of all kinds
- Cantaloupe
- Cherries
- Grapefruit
- Grapes
- Honeydew
- Kiwi
- Lemon *(used in cooking or dressings)*
- Lime *(again for cooking or dressings)*
- Nectarine
- Orange
- Peach
- Pear
- Pineapple
- Tangerine
- Tomatoes
- Watermelon

THE TRUTH ABOUT WATER

- About 75 percent of Americans are chronically dehydrated and this likely applies to half of the world's population.

- In 37 percent of Americans, the thirst mechanism is so weak that it is often mistaken for hunger.

- Even mild dehydration will slow down one's metabolism by as much as 3 percent.

- One glass of water shuts down midnight hunger pangs for almost 100 percent of the dieters studied in a University of Washington study.

- A lack of water is the number one trigger of daytime fatigue.

- Preliminary research indicates that drinking eight to ten glasses of water a day could significantly ease back and joint pain for up to 80 percent of sufferers.

- A mere 2 percent drop in body water can trigger fuzzy short-term memory, trouble with basic math, and difficulty focusing on the computer screen or on a printed page.

- Drinking five glasses of water daily decreases the risk of colon cancer by 45 percent, plus it can slash the risk of breast cancer by 79 percent, and one is 50 percent less likely to develop bladder cancer.

- Your body uses approximately 150 calories to heat a gallon of refrigerator cold water to 98.6 degrees (body temperature) in order to void it, so if you want to lose fat faster superhydrate!

Water and Your Child's Body

How important is water to your child? Well, consider that our bodies range anywhere from 50 to 65 percent water, and some experts say it's even more. Without water we can live for only a few days or perhaps more and that's about that. As the saying goes "You are what you eat," but you are also what you drink as well.

Not all body parts have the same amount of water. Here's the basic breakdown:

- Blood: 90 percent water

- Brain: 85 percent water

- Muscle: 75 percent water

- Skin: 71 percent water

- Bone: 30 percent water

- Body fat: 15 percent water

Seems like the body finds water fairly important, no? Clearly, if you don't drink enough water, you will slowly but surely become dehydrated. As your body experiences dehydration, you'll more than likely feel it first in those areas that contain the most water.

For example, at first you lose alertness and feel fuzzy in your head. Next, you'll suffer from total body muscular fatigue. As you can see from the chart, dead last is how dehydration affects your fat. And why is this important? Well, most of us and especially overfat children need to lose fat. So the idea that excessive sweating is good for fat loss makes little physiological sense. In fact, staying cool burns many more calories than keeping warm, and all without the water loss.

Water is actually a type of food. You may not think of it this way, but it's the most important nutritional necessity in your eating plan. As I mentioned before, you can't live very long without it.

So that you can see the importance of water, here is a short list of the many purposes water serves in your body:

- Acts as a solvent for vitamins, minerals, amino acids, and glucose

- Transports vital nutrients

- Aids in the digestion of food

- Lubricates your joints

- Serves as a type of shock absorber inside the eyes and spinal cord

- Helps regulate and maintain body temperature

- Rids the body of waste products (and fat!) through the urine

- Disseminates heat through the skin, lungs, and urine

- Keeps your skin supple and elastic

- Assists in intense muscular contraction

In short, water is a vital and critically important aspect of your child's daily eating regimen. Try using flavored waters that contain no sugar to get your child to drink more.

Warning: Partial Dehydration

If you are aware and sensitive enough to your and your child's body, you should be able to recognize some of the early warnings of partial dehydration. Here are the symptoms of partial dehydration:

- Dizziness

- Headaches

- Fatigue

- Thirst

- Flushed skin

- Blurred vision

- Muscle weakness

Many people—even sports coaches—wait too long to hydrate, sometimes allowing for these symptoms to occur. It is one of the reasons that sports teams use sports drinks like

Gatorade to make water tasty to drink. Offering these tastier alternatives ensures that athletes will more readily stay hydrated. Unfortunately, most people, even athletes, never realize that they spend most days in a state of partial dehydration. In fact, some experts suggest that long before you are thirsty, you are already somewhat dehydrated.

Flushing Out the Fat

Water aids the fat-loss process in many ways. One of the most important is in allowing the internal organs to function properly. For example, your kidneys need sufficient water to function properly. If they don't get enough water, your liver actually takes over and performs some of the functions of the kidneys. This can shortchange your liver's most important task, which is to eat up stored fat and covert it into fuel. So if you want to maximize the metabolism of your and your child's fat stores, water is your "bestest" friend. (I love it when kids say that!)

Axing the Appetite

Pee-Pee Power. When you lose fat, where does it go? It doesn't just fall off your body and bounce on the floor. Neither does it leap off your belly into the trash bin. Any ideas? Well, here's the skinny on fat—most of your fat is lost as heat from your skin. Yep, right off the old epidermis. The two other ways you discard fat is out with your breath and when you urinate.

There seems to be a lot of anecdotal evidence from friends of mine who own and run gyms that drinking copious amounts of water curbs the appetite.

Ellington Darden, Ph.D., has written more than 40 books on the subject of diet and strength training. He is a good friend and has successfully helped thousands of people lose fat and gain muscle. Darden has used what he calls superhydration (drinking about a gallon of water a day) many times to help speed fat loss and improve health. As Darden explains:

Superhydration can double, triple, or even quadruple your urine production. As a result, you'll be able to eliminate more heat. Remember, inside your body, fat loss means heat loss. So get used to going to the bathroom more frequently than normal.

And the colder the water the better! When you drink cold water, your body has to heat it to your normal body temperature of 98.6 degrees. According to Darden, it takes about one calorie to heat one ounce of water to the body's core temperature. So an 8-ounce glass of cold water burns approximately 8 calories. So if you extend that over 16 glasses, meaning drinking one full gallon of H_2O, your body uses up an additional 123 calories! Not too shabby!

Another way to help this acclimation is to sip instead of gulp. Goofy straws of all different types or thermoses that have cool characters make it more fun for kids to drink.

Cure for Constipation

Another one of the many functions of water is to help prevent constipation. Superhydration makes it much easier for you and your child if bowel movements are an issue. There is no need to use stool-softening drugs—just pull out the filtered water and drink.

Purified Water vs. Tap

Many experts claim that most water that comes from cities, especially in apartment buildings, is tainted. It could be that there is too much metal or too many minerals (perhaps from old building pipes), but unless you have your water profession-ally tested, I certainly cannot tell you what is best. At home we use a Culligan reverse osmosis system that removes just about everything from the water, which can be good but can also be bad.

When it comes to this matter, it is best to do some homework on the subject. Google "water purification" and instead of watching your favorite TV show tonight, take this time to educate yourself on the subject so that you can make an intelligent choice. Whatever system you choose—reverse osmosis, purification, or good old tap water—drink cool or cold water and in large amounts. Put a couple of bottles in your child's backpack and reward her for drinking them with a low-carb cookie! (See the recipe section for a great low-carb cookie recipe.)

So, are you and your children drinking the amount of water you should every day? Seltzer or club soda is fine as well. A little squeeze of lemon or lime in your water is a good way to make it more pleasurable. A great book on the subject is *Your Body's Many Cries for Water* by Fereydoon Batmanghelidj.

Conclusion

Our children are our legacy. Giving them the very best in exercise and nutrition should not be an afterthought. It should be what concerns us most and what we strive for on a daily basis. Myths and misinformation abound in exercise and nutrition. As an adult, believing in the many myths after learning the truths are up to you. Kids don't get to choose. They rely on you for the correct information. What you have just read is grounded in current science and in my personal experience as a fitness professional.

I hope that you find ways to incorporate 30 minutes of strength training, ideally in the way I have laid out in this book, and an improved way of eating into you and your child's life starting today—starting now at your very next meal. And rather than saying, "Just do it," I say, "Just do it and do it right." I know that it's hard. I know that it's a challenge. I know that it can be uncomfortable. But at the same time it is remarkably rewarding and tremendously satisfying. I guarantee it.

But heck, why listen to me? Take it from G.B. Shaw:

> Forget about likes and dislike. They are of no consequence. Just do what must be done. This may not be happiness, but it is greatness.

Or maybe Shakespeare:

O! 'Tis excellent to have a giant's strength!

As mentioned on page 17, I invite you to visit my websites and web forums at www.SeriousStrength.com and www.StrongKidsHealthyKids.com where you can participate in discussions and where I will personally answer your questions and concerns.

Truly yours in strength for health!

—Fred Hahn

Case Studies

BRIAN HAMMER

Before I tell you about a great kid named Brian Hammer
and the tremendous ongoing transformation he's experienced,
I'd like you to hear what his parents have to say about their
experience with Slow Burn:

> Before meeting Fred and learning about Serious Strength
> and Slow Burn, we were at a loss to help our son Brian.
> After taking a prescription medication for several months,
> Brian had gained close to 50 pounds. For a ten-year-old child,
> a weight gain of that magnitude is not only scary and
> overwhelming, but it also posed serious health concerns.
> For almost two years, we tried to help Brian lose the weight
> by exercising and cutting calories. No matter how hard we
> and he tried, he couldn't rid himself of the weight.
>
> For a child with self-esteem issues and learning disabili-
> ties, and for us as parents, we were living a nightmare.
> Brian became more angry and depressed; he was embar-
> rassed and miserable with his appearance. As his parents
> we felt helpless, not knowing where to turn.
>
> Learning about Serious Strength and the Slow Burn
> method was a turning point for our entire family. Fred Hahn

and Brian's trainer Tommy Day became our saviors. Everything we had been taught in the past about hours of aerobic exercise and calorie counting being the solution was forgotten. Brian began a once-a-week 30-minute Slow Burn training session, along with a high-protein eating program, and within a couple of weeks, the pounds started to come off.

At first Brian was uncooperative. The program, as we called it, wasn't easy for him and he had become quite jaded after his previous unsuccessful attempts to lose weight. But he kept with it, and with his trainer's patience and persistence, Brian experienced his first significant results in years. With this new motivation, Brian became empowered to work harder and he became committed to the program with a vigor we could never have imagined. Brian went to school and bragged to his friends and teachers about how great he was doing with his program. The eating and exercise routine became part of his life and he stopped complaining about not eating the foods he used to crave.

After a few months on the program, Brian's self-esteem is tremendous. His face beams when his friends, family, and teachers comment on his quite obvious weight loss. More important, Brian feels better about himself. He can move more easily, and he feels stronger and more able to participate and compete in sports and other physical activities. He has learned to like himself again and his confidence in himself has been restored. He is wearing clothes he hasn't fit into in years. He wants to shop for new clothes every chance he gets!

The staff at Brian's school has also seen the huge strides Brian has made. His attention and focus difficulties at school have decreased along with his behavioral and social problems. As he shed his unwanted pounds, he regained self-confidence and self-esteem. He has reclaimed his position as a leader among his peers and his attention and focus have improved significantly. Brian has been described by his teachers as "happier than ever" and "empowered, proud, and confident."

Brian still has a way to go but we have no doubt he will reach his goals. Fred, Tom, and Serious Strength have given us the greatest gift of all—they have helped Brian regain his happiness, confidence, self-esteem, motivation, and health. They have given us our son back.

Thank you from the bottom of our hearts.

—Michael and Lisa Hammer

Here is a copy of Brian's body composition report. The device we use is a sophisticated bioimpedance machine that measures total body water and converts the information into an accurate picture of a person's lean-mass to fat-mass ratio. Next to the expensive method of hydrostatic (under water) weighing, which is the gold standard in body fat/lean mass testing, a total body bioimpedance machine like the one we use at Serious Strength is the next best thing out there for determining body composition, meaning the amount of fat tissue and lean tissue (e.g., muscle, bone, etc.) on a person's body.

Brian's first body composition test was taken on April 9, 2007:

Health Management Program
ELG Data Report

Client Data

Impedance: 544	Height: 54.00	Sex: Male
Age: 11	Weight: 155.00	

Lean Body Mass

Weight of Lean Body Mass: 89.69 lbs

Percentage of Lean Body Mass: 57.9%

Lean Body Mass to Fat Ratio: 1.4 to 1

Total Body Water: 30.7 liters

Fat Free Mass is composed of muscles, body fluid, connective tissue, and bones. The optimal **Lean to Fat** ratio for you is at least 5.1 to 1.

Body Fat

Weight of Body Fat: 65.31 lbs

Percentage of Body Fat: 42.1%

Fat is calories stored as energy reserve for your body. The desired range of percentage **Body Fat** for you is **8–14%** (or 7–14 lbs). If you consume more calories than your body burns, the excess calories are stored as **Body Fat**. Excess **Body Fat** "frequently results in a significant impairment of health."

Current Status & Goals

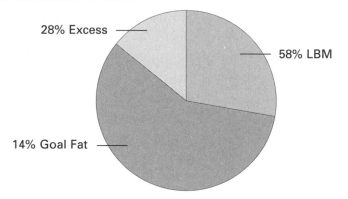

The graph above shows your current body composition. **"LBM"** represents our **Lean Body Mass** and includes all body components except fat. **"Goal Fat"** represents **Goal Body Fat,** which is necessary for proper physical health. **"Excess"** is **Fat** that is in excess of normal limits, and is unhealthy.

Your Goal: 104 lbs (14.0% Fat)

Your goal on the **Health Management Program** will be to lose **Excess Body Fat**. Optimizing your body composition will help you lose those extra pounds, make you feel better, and will promote a healthier style of living. The National Institutes of Health (NIH) estimates that more than 60% of the adult population is overweight. More than 30% are obese, a disease that can dramatically increase risk of cardiovascular disease, cancer, diabetes, and hypertension.

The next report was just one month later:

Health Management Program
ELG Data Report

Client Data

Impedance: 557	Height: 54.00	Sex: Male
Age: 11	Weight: 144.00	

Lean Body Mass

Weight of Lean Body Mass: 87.94 lbs

Percentage of Lean Body Mass: 61.1%

Lean Body Mass to Fat Ratio: 1.6 to 1

Total Body Water: 29.3 liters

Fat Free Mass is composed of muscles, body fluid, connective tissue, and bones. The optimal **Lean to Fat** ratio for you is at least 5.1 to 1.

Body Fat

Weight of Body Fat: 56.06 lbs

Percentage of Body Fat: 38.9%

Fat is calories stored as energy reserve for your body. The desired range of percentage **Body Fat** for you is **8–14%** (or 7–14 lbs). If you consume more calories than your body burns, the excess calories are stored as **Body Fat**. Excess **Body Fat** "frequently results in a significant impairment of health."

Current Status & Goals

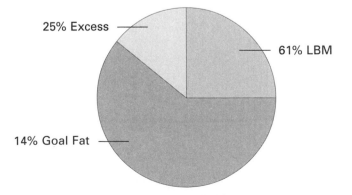

The graph above shows your current body composition. **"LBM"** represents our **Lean Body Mass** and includes all body components except fat. **"Goal Fat"** represents **Goal Body Fat,** which is necessary for proper physical health. **"Excess"** is **Fat** that is in excess of normal limits, and is unhealthy.

Your Goal: 102 lbs (14.0% Fat)

Your goal on the **Health Management Program** will be to lose **Excess Body Fat.** Optimizing your body composition will help you lose those extra pounds, make you feel better, and will promote a healthier style of living. The National Institutes of Health (NIH) estimates that more than 60% of the adult population is overweight. More than 30% are obese, a disease that can dramatically increase risk of cardiovascular disease, cancer, diabetes, and hypertension.

You can see from the second report that Brian lost 9.25 pounds of fat and reduced his body fat percentage from 42.1 percent to 38.9 percent—in just one month. The slight loss of lean mass was due to his loss of body water from 30.7 liters to 29.9 liters. A liter of water weighs 2.2 pounds. So since he lost 1.4 liters of water, the machine thinks he lost 3.08 pounds of lean. But he didn't. He lost only 1.75 pounds of lean, which means he actually gained. Hydration levels fluctuate over the course of the day so this difference is fairly normal. But the important issue is the significant amount of fat he lost in just a month.

Here is Brian's most recent report conducted several months later:

Health Management Program
ELG Data Report

Client Data

Impedance: 543	Height: 54.20	Sex: Male
Age: 12	Weight: 135.00	

Lean Body Mass

> Weight of Lean Body Mass: 90.14 lbs
>
> Percentage of Lean Body Mass: 66.8%
>
> Lean Body Mass to Fat Ratio: 2.0 to 1

Total Body Water: 29.0 liters

Fat Free Mass is composed of muscles, body fluid, connective tissue, and bones. The optimal **Lean to Fat** ratio for you is at least 5.1 to 1.

Body Fat

Weight of Body Fat: 44.86 lbs

Percentage of Body Fat: 33.2%

Fat is calories stored as energy reserve for your body. The desired range of percentage **Body Fat** for you is **8–14%** (or 7–14 lbs). If you consume more calories than your body burns, the excess calories are stored as **Body Fat**. Excess **Body Fat** "frequently results in a significant impairment of health."

Current Status & Goals

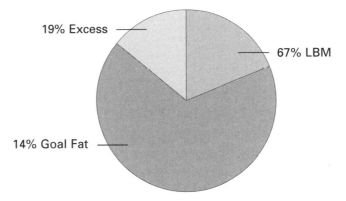

The graph above shows your current body composition. **"LBM"** represents our **Lean Body Mass** and includes all body components except fat. **"Goal Fat"** represents **Goal Body Fat,** which is necessary for proper physical health. **"Excess"** is **Fat** that is in excess of normal limits, and is unhealthy.

Your Goal: 105 lbs (14.0% Fat)

Your goal on the **Health Management Program** will be to lose **Excess Body Fat**. Optimizing your body composition will help you lose those extra pounds, make you feel better, and will promote a healthier style of living. The National Institutes of Health (NIH) estimates that more than 60% of the adult population is overweight. More than 30% are obese, a disease that can dramatically increase risk of cardiovascular disease, cancer, diabetes, and hypertension.

In roughly 32 weeks (a total of 30 half-hour exercise sessions), Brian has lost 21 pounds of fat, decreased his body fat percentage from 42 percent to 32 percent, and is well over 50 percent stronger in all of his exercises. Had Brian come more regularly and been a bit better in his eating habits, his results would have been far better. But the most important thing is how much happier and alert Brian has become and that he is on the fast track to reaching his goal.

ALEX S.

Alex came to us at age 14 weighing 213 pounds. He was very tall for his age (almost 5 feet 10 inches) and heading toward severe clinical obesity. His mother really wanted to help him and we assured her we could help.

He started the program on June 6, 2000, but only came in once that month. He skipped July entirely, came once again in August, once yet again in September and then on October 7, 2000, came in weighing 231 pounds.

He then came in three times in October, twice in November (due to Thanksgiving holidays), three times in December (also holidays), three times in January, and once in February.

At this point, he still weighed in at 231 pounds. However, you could see that the added muscle tissue was changing his body. Although he was looking and feeling much better, he still needed to get more serious with his attendance as well as his eating habits. I read him the riot act and he restarted his effort in earnest.

Ten months later, in 2001, he weighed in at 218. Losing 13 pounds in ten months doesn't sound like much until you realize that he was also growing.

Alex continued his progress:

On January 5, 2002, he weighed 200.

On April 27, 2002, he weighed 194.

On February 8, 2003, he weighed 180.

On May 4, 2003, he weighed 169.

Bear in mind that all the while Alex was growing in height, which meant he should have been getting heavier, not lighter. He was a little over 6 feet 2 inches at the last weigh-in. Alex did not want his before and pictures published in this book so we only listed his measurement changes:

Before	**After**
Age: 14	Age: 17
Weight: 213 lbs	Weight: 169 lbs
Height: 5'10"	Height: 6'2"

MICHAEL H.

At 5 feet 3 inches tall, 12-year-old Michael weighed 145.5 pounds when he first arrived at my Serious Strength studio. He was a quiet and shy young man, but sedentary? Not in the least. Michael was, in fact, an active athlete; he played soccer and basketball regularly. Michael began to train with me twice weekly—sometimes only once—for 15 minutes at each session. He performed approximately eight strength exercises and no aerobic activity at all. After eight months of slow speed strength training, Mike was more confident and better at his sports. He scored more points for his basketball team in one game than all his other teammates combined. As for his fat, 32 pounds had melted away until he weighed a mere 113 pounds—despite growing two inches.

Before

Age: 12

Weight: 145.5 lbs

Height: 5'3"

After

Age: 13

Weight: 113 lbs

Height: 5'5"

Kid-Ready Recipes

The following recipes were created by various clients (and my wife who is also a client of sorts) and are pretty darn delicious! Try them on your kids. They are healthful and I do believe they'll find many of them scrumdilicious!

CARSON GLEBERMAN'S RECIPES

DISCOVERY TEAM BARS

1   stick butter, room temperature

1/4   cup dark brown sugar

1/2   cup dark molasses
      (Plantation Blackstrap has more iron than other brands)

1   egg

1/2   cup peanut butter

1/2   teaspoon baking soda

1/4   teaspoon salt

1   teaspoon vanilla extract

1   scoop GNC whey protein

2/3   cup nonfat dry milk powder (about half an envelope)

1/4   cup flaxseed meal (available at health-food stores)

3/4   cup flour

1   cup quick-cooking oatmeal (but not instant) or steel cut
      quick-cooking for a bumpier texture (steel cut regular will be
      unpleasant)

1/2   cup dried cranberries (or dried blueberries or cherries or raisins)

4   ounces fine-quality dark chocolate, chopped and separated into
      two equal piles

1. Preheat oven to 350 degrees F.

2. Unwrap butter, use wrapper to grease two 8 x 8 square baking pans.

3. Mix together butter, sugar, and molasses on low speed till uniform.

4. Add remaining ingredients except for one pile of chopped chocolate. Batter will be stiff and glossy.

5. Divide evenly into pans, and spread out to make the tops level.

6. Bake about 12 to 18 minutes, until the edges look a shade darker and roll away from the sides of the pan. Cake tester will come out clean or with dry crumbs unless you hit a melted chocolate chip. (If you have a convection oven, only bake about 10 minutes at 350 degrees.)

7. Sprinkle the reserved pile of chopped chocolate evenly across tops of pans. Spread chocolate with knife or spatula as it melts to make an even coating. This takes a little patience and a few minutes. Cool completely on racks (chocolate will no longer be shiny).

8. Cut each pan into 8 bars. Wrap each piece in waxed paper like brownies. Store in the refrigerator.

CREAMED SPINACH

4   tablespoons butter

1   small onion or 1/2 large onion, minced very fine (part of the trick is including the taste of onion without the kids being able to identify pieces of it)

Several pinches of salt

1 1/2   tablespoons flour (can't substitute here)

1/3   cup milk

1   pound spinach, washed twice and de-stemmed, spun or toweled dry

Several tablespoons grated parmesan, or more

Black pepper to taste

1. Melt butter in large saucepan.

2. Sauté onion with one pinch of salt over medium low heat until dark yellow (a few small pieces will be brown).

3. Meanwhile, chop the spinach coarsely.

4. Add the flour to the onion-butter mixture and stir until foamy.

5. Add half the milk and stir until the mixture thickens; add the rest of the milk and repeat.

6. Now add the spinach and another generous pinch of salt. Turn down the heat and stir continuously until the spinach starts to give up its liquid. The sauce will get much thinner at this point, but continue to cook, stirring occasionally until it thickens up again.

7. Add cheese and pepper and serve.

EGGPLANT GOAT CHEESE ROLLS

3	small Japanese eggplants
4	ounces goat cheese
1–2	tablespoons fresh herbs such as tarragon, rosemary, or dill
3	tablespoons olive oil
	Wooden toothpicks
	Balsamic vinegar (optional)

1. Wash eggplants.

2. Slice with a mandolin diagonally so that you get long, narrow, thin slices.

3. Chop herbs, add a pinch of pepper (optional) to the goat cheese. (Any leftover herbed goat cheese will inspire its own uses.)

4. Put a small amount of herbed goat cheese at one end of an eggplant slice, and roll up toward the other. Secure the end with a toothpick. The exact amount of cheese depends on the width of your eggplants, but maybe a half tablespoon to a tablespoon will be right.

5. Repeat with all slices.

6. Heat enough olive oil to cover the bottom of your skillet, then put the rolls in. You can put them close to each other, but if they don't fit, you can do the last ones in a second batch while the first ones rest in a warm oven.

7. Turn them over when golden, after approximately 4 minutes. If you do a second batch, you will need more oil.

8. You can drizzle a tiny bit of balsamic vinegar on them, or use it for dipping, or just eat them as is. They make nice appetizers.

CAULIFLOWER AU GRATIN

1	head cauliflower
4	cups water to parboil in a 2-quart saucepan
2	tablespoons butter
1	tablespoon flour
1/2	cup milk
3/4	cup grated Gruyère cheese
1/4	cup grated sharp cheddar cheese
2	tablespoons grated Parmesan cheese
2	tablespoons breadcrumbs, or mixture of breadcrumbs and hazelnut flour

1. Cut cauliflower into small florets.

2. Heat enough water to cover them well to boiling, dunk florets in for 1 minute, then drain.

3. Preheat oven to 350 degrees F.

4. Butter an oven-safe casserole dish and put cauliflower in.

5. In a medium saucepan, melt the butter. Add the flour and whisk gently until it becomes foamy.

6. Add the milk in thirds, stirring in between until thick.

7. Turn off the heat, add the Gruyère and cheddar and stir until uniform. Pour over the cauliflower.

8. Bake for about 20 minutes, until it is bubbly. Remove from oven. Keep dish covered to keep warm.

9. Preheat your broiler.

10. Mix the Parmesan and breadcrumbs. Spread mixture over top of dish. Put dish under broiler just for a minute or two to brown and crisp the top.

CRISPY GREENS

1   bunch (1 pound) collards, kale, turnip greens, beet greens, chard, spinach, or some combination

2   cloves garlic, sliced

2   slices bacon (optional)

2   tablespoons olive oil

     Pinch of salt

     Pinch of black or red pepper

1.   Wash greens well. Spin in salad spinner or roll in dishtowel to dry.

2.   If you have a combination that includes both beefy greens (collards, kale, turnip greens) and more delicate ones (beet greens, spinach, chard), separate the former from the latter.

3.   Stack large leaves on a cutting board, roll, and slice into very thin ribbons.

4.   If you are using bacon, cook it in a skillet over medium low heat, until just crispy. Remove slices and set aside.

5.   Including bacon fat and olive oil, start with about 2 tablespoons of fat in your skillet.

6.   Over medium heat, cook the garlic 1 minute. Add the beefy textured greens and some salt.

7.   If you like them a little spicy, add a pinch of crushed red pepper or a generous grinding of black pepper.

8.   Sauté, turning over with a spoon until wilted.

9.   Add more delicate greens and continue sautéing and turning over until the greens begin to get crisp. They will have reduced in volume considerably, but not in taste.

10. Chop the bacon, add back in, and serve.

SESAME-MISO CARROTS

(You can use broccoli florets, zucchini [don't overcook], green beans, snow peas, asparagus, etc., in this recipe instead of carrots.)

1   **bunch carrots**

2   **tablespoons butter**

1   **tablespoon soy sauce**

1   **tablespoon sesame oil**

1   **tablespoon white miso**

2   **tablespoons toasted sesame seeds**

Chopped dill (optional)

1. Clean carrots, peel if needed, and cut lengthwise into pieces as big around as your little finger.

2. Cut crosswise into 1-inch pieces.

3. Melt butter in saucepan and sauté carrots slowly over medium low heat until soft but still a little crisp.

4. In a small bowl, mix the soy sauce, sesame oil, and miso. You can add a little warm water if it seems lumpy. Add this to the carrots and just heat through (you can't let miso get too hot or its texture becomes unattractive).

5. Sprinkle sesame seeds on top and serve.

FALAFEL

1/4   **cup coarse kashi (bulgar wheat)**

1/2   **cup water or broth**

      Big handful parsley leaves

1/2   **onion**

  1   **egg**

  1   **can garbanzo beans, drained**

  1   **lemon, juice and grated zest**

      Splash olive oil

1/4   **teaspoon salt**

1/4   **teaspoon ground cumin**

      Pinch of hyssop (optional)

      Olive oil for sautéing, or peanut oil for deep frying

1. Over medium heat, bring the kashi and water or broth just to a boil. Lower heat and stir and simmer until liquid is absorbed (5 minutes or so).

2. In a food processor, pulse the onion, parsley, and egg until quite fine. Add the remaining ingredients (except olive oil) and pulse briefly. Mixture should be uniform but medium coarse.

3. Heat oil for sautéing (our preference) or frying.

4. Form mixture into balls or little patties and sauté or fry. (We've tried baking and can't recommend it.) You are aiming for crispy outside but not dried out inside. A little underdone is better than overdone.

5. Cool slightly on paper towels.

6. Serve with tahini, mango chutney, ketchup, salsa, or green Indian cilantro sauce for dipping. Leftovers can be reheated in a 300-degree oven, but the microwave is not kind to falafel.

HUDSON VALLEY ROAST PORK LOIN

1	small onion
2	small tart apples
1/4	cup cranberries (heaping)
	Olive oil
1 1/2–2	pounds pork loin
1/4	teaspoon salt
1/4	teaspoon pepper
6	sage leaves, chopped fine or 1/2 to 1 teaspoon dried sage, to taste
1/4	cup white wine

1. Preheat oven to 400 degrees F.

2. Put a couple of teaspoons of olive oil on the bottom of a metal roasting pan and spread out across the bottom.

3. Slice the onion in very thin rings and sprinkle over the bottom of the pan.

4. Peel, core, and slice the apples thin and layer those on top. Add the cranberries.

5. I usually find I need to untie the loin and trim more fat off than the butcher did, then re-roll and tie the roast. But don't be too compulsive—a little fat does this dish good!

6. Rub the retied roast with a little more olive oil, then salt, pepper, and sage. Place on top of onion and fruit. Cover with foil.

7. Bake about 40 to 45 minutes in a convection oven, 10 or 15 minutes longer in a regular oven—until a meat thermometer in center says 160 degrees. (Note: It will take about an hour in a regular oven [convection shortens the

time by about a third], but I would recommend checking after 50 minutes. It depends on how thick the thickest part of the loin is because two roasts of exactly the same weight can take different cooking times. If you don't have a meat thermometer, you can check by sticking the point of a knife into the thickest part of the loin and seeing if the juices run clear and the inside looks light pink— definitely not red, but not yet beige. It will cook a little more during the resting period. Because the steam stays in the foil, the roast is not in danger of drying out, so if in doubt, bake for 5 minutes more and check again.)

8. Remove roast to cutting board to rest 10 minutes.

9. Meanwhile, take out baked fruit and onion with slotted spoon to serve as a confit with the slices of roast pork.

10. Put roasting pan over a burner on medium low heat and deglaze with wine, mashing and stirring to dissolve as many of the little bits as possible. Taste this gravy and adjust seasoning if necessary.

11. Slice the roast and serve with confit and gravy.

   (This is really good with a nice lentil dish, quinoa, wild rice, or black-eyed peas, plus a salad with edgy greens like arugula or endive.)

PARMESAN CHICKEN BREASTS OR TOFU

1	pound chicken breast and/or firm tofu but soft or silken will work in this recipe as long as the pieces stay 2 inches x 3 inches x 1/2 inch
3	tablespoons grated Parmesan cheese
1 1/2	teaspoons chopped fresh herbs (a mix of tarragon and marjoram is good, or rosemary and parsley, or just a little bit of sage and a lot of chives)
1/4	cup whole-wheat flour or oat flour
1	tablespoon flax seed meal
1	scant teaspoon mustard powder
1/4	teaspoon salt
1/4	teaspoon pepper
	Olive oil
	Lemon wedges or balsamic vinegar

1. Cut chicken into cutlet pieces about 1/4 to 1/2 inch thick. For tofu, make 1/2-inch-thick slices no bigger than 3 inches by 2 inches (so they don't fall apart when you turn them).

2. On a plate, mix together the Parmesan cheese, herbs, flour, flax seed meal, mustard powder, salt, and pepper. Dredge the cutlets in this mixture to coat very lightly.

3. Heat olive oil in a skillet and sauté chicken pieces until just dark golden on either side—about 5 minutes on the first side, maybe 3 minutes on the second side.

4. Serve with a squeeze of lemon or a thin drizzle of balsamic vinegar.

LISA FELDMAN'S COTTAGE CHEESE AND PEANUT BUTTER BREAKFAST

(The world's fastest, most well-balanced breakfast)

1⁄2   **cup Friendship Whipped Cottage Cheese***

1   **tablespoon chunky natural peanut or almond butter (softened out of the fridge for about 10 minutes)**

2   **large chopped-up prunes or 1 scant tablespoon of raisins (for a dessert or special treat version, you can use mini-chocolate chips)**

Place all the ingredients in a small serving bowl and mix everything together with a spoon. Sweeten to taste. Eat from the same bowl with the same spoon—just like cereal!

*One of the things that makes this so appealing to kids (as well as adults) is its smooth texture due to the whipped curdless cottage cheese. To the best of my knowledge, only Friendship makes this kind of product (it is 1% fat). If it is not available at your local store, the same effect can be achieved by pulsing regular cottage cheese in a food processor for a minute or so. You can also use a mixing bowl and hand blender to make medium curd cottage cheese smoother.

LINDA HAHN'S RECIPES

THE BEST BROCCOLI

One bunch of broccoli (I estimate at least four spears per kid)

Kosher salt

1 to 2 tablespoons unsalted organic butter (more or less)

I make fresh broccoli for my children nearly every night. It is their favorite vegetable and I can be reasonably certain that they will eat it. Though, if they are served broccoli anywhere else, say at a friend's home or at a restaurant, they may try it, but they usually leave it on the plate with the excuse that it does not taste like the broccoli at home. When the same friends come to our home for dinner, the broccoli bowl is always empty. Georgia's friend Jamie claims that I make "the best" broccoli.

Broccoli is tricky because if it is not fresh or if it is over-cooked for even a minute, it just doesn't taste good (not to mention that most of the nutritional value has been cooked out of it). If it is undercooked, well, at least my kids won't eat it because it is too tough. Not all kids are that picky, but if you've tried to feed your kids broccoli and they've turned their noses up at it, maybe it's not the broccoli that's the problem. It just might be the cooking technique.

First, you need to buy fresh and preferably organic broccoli. During the summer, I love getting locally grown broccoli at the farmer's market. Talk about fresh. When I'm faced with buying broccoli at the grocery store, I will opt for fresh over organic if it looks like the organic has been sitting around for ages. You can tell when broccoli is fresh when the florets are a deep green and tight and the bottoms of the stalk where it was cut looks moist and not dried out. If the florets are floppy or yellowish don't buy it. It won't taste good. When that happens— no fresh broccoli to be found—I buy frozen organic.

1. Get a pot with a steamer insert or a steamer basket that fits into it so that the lid still fits tightly.

2. Put an inch or so of water into the pot, making sure the basket sits above the water. Boil the water with the lid on.

3. Cut the florets into bite-size pieces. If you leave the stems long, you can later play that you're eating broccoli lollipops. I'll cut up the stalks too after trimming off the tough outer layer, steam them along with the florets, and eat them myself. Once the water is rapidly boiling, lift the lid and put the broccoli into the steamer basket. Replace the lid, trying not to let all the steam escape.

4. Now, here's the real trick. Set a timer. Steam the broccoli for 5 minutes—no more, no less. When the timer rings, take off the heat immediately and put the broccoli into a lidded serving bowl (or use a plate as a lid).

5. Sprinkle liberally with kosher salt and dot with butter.

6. Put the lid on the bowl and let sit for a moment. When the butter has melted, swirl the broccoli in the melted butter. Serve immediately or let cool a bit for younger kids.

Variations: Some kids might like a cheese sauce on their broccoli. Or you might try squeezing some lemon juice and olive oil on it instead of butter.

This steaming technique works for many different vegetables. I use it for asparagus, cauliflower, and string beans. The only thing you have to do is experiment with the amount of time you need to steam these vegetables. I have found that string beans and cauliflower also take 5 minutes. Steaming time for asparagus will vary with the thickness—from 3 to 7 minutes.

NANI PANCAKES

2   **large eggs (preferably from organically or pasture-raised chickens)**

1   **generous pinch of kosher salt**

4   **tablespoons flour (I use organic whole-grain pastry flour)**

1/8   **cup half and half (preferably organic)**

1/8   **cup (or a bit more) whole milk (preferably organic)**

Butter for cooking

Sugar, jam, real maple syrup, semi-sweet chocolate chips, or any other healthy sweetener for the filling

This recipe makes 2 pancakes in a 10-inch non-stick skillet

Serving a hot, well-balanced breakfast to my children, especially on school mornings, has been almost like a calling for me ever since they started preschool. I am pulled out of my warm bed every morning by the memories of my own childhood when I entered the kitchen before school and my mother would offer a warm, nourishing breakfast. My favorite was her Lithuanian-style pancakes (blynai), which are a lot like a French crepe. My children call them Nani pancakes after my mother. (She was named Nani by Alex, her first grandchild, because he loved the bananas—nanas—she would prepare for him.) It is very likely that my mother did not ponder the nutrient content of the breakfasts she made for us, but instinctively she always included healthy sources of protein and fat—eggs, bacon, and whole milk—knowing that these foods would keep us better satisfied while in school. Over the years with my children, I have revised this pancake recipe to skew higher in the protein and fat content, adding just enough flour to keep the pancakes from falling apart in the pan. When it's all said and done, the kids are off to school with at least one whole egg in them to sustain their bodies and brains until lunch.

Here's how I make them.

1. Warm the skillet over medium heat.

2. Crack two eggs into a medium-size bowl and whisk together with the salt.

3. Add the flour and whisk until all lumps are gone.

4. Whisk in the half and half and then the milk.

5. Add enough butter to the pan to generously coat the bottom to keep the pancake from sticking. The pan should be hot enough to instantly melt the butter but it should not brown.

6. Pour in half of the batter.

7. Carefully flip over when it has completely set (after 3 or 4 minutes).

8. Let cook another minute or so.

9. Slide out onto a plate.

10. Re-whisk the remaining batter, add a little more butter to the pan, and pour in remaining batter. When the pancakes are done, add whatever healthy sweetener your child likes. They won't need much because it becomes a sweet and savory combination that is always satisfying without adding too much of either.

11. Roll or fold the pancake in any way that pleases your child or leave it flat on the plate.

Variation: Just like a French crepe, these pancakes can be made as a base for a ham and cheese rollup, or anything else you can think of!

Endnotes

Introduction

1. Westcott, et al. "School Based Conditioning Programs for Physically Unfit Children," *Strength and Conditioning* 17 (1995): 5–9.

2. Ramsden, et al., *Specialized Strength Training* (Monterey, Calif.: Exercise Science Publishers, 2001).

3. Morris, et al., "Prospective Ten-Month Exercise Intervention in Premenarchael Girls: Positive Effects on Bone and Lean Mass," *Journal of Bone and Mineral Research* 12, no. 9 (1997): 1453–1462.

4. A.D. Faigenbaum, et al., "The Effects of Twice-a-Week Strength Training Program on Children," *Pediatric Exercise Science* 5 (1993): 339–346.

5. A.D. Faigenbaum, "Strength Training for Children and Adolescents," *Clinical Sports Medicine* 19, no. 4 (October 2000): 593–619.

6. Laura K. Smith, Elizabeth Lawrence Weiss, and L. Don Lehmkuhl, *Brumstrom's Clinical Kinesiology* 5th ed. (Philadelphia: F.A. Davis Co., 1996), 142.

7. Westcott, et al. "Effects of Regular and Slow Speed Resistance Training on Muscle Strength," *Journal of Sports Medicine and Physical Fitness* 41 (2001): 154–158.

8. W.W. Cambell, M.C. Crim, V.R. Young, and W.J. Evans, "Increased Energy Requirements and Changes in Body Composition with Resistance Training in Older Adults," *American Journal of Clinical Nutrition,* 60, no. 2 (August 1994): 167–175.

9. R. Pratley, et al., "Strength Training Increases Resting Metabolic Rate and Norepinephrine Levels in Healthy 50–65 Year Old Men," *Journal of Applied Physiology,* 76, no. 1 (January 2008): 133–137.

Chapter 1

1. Guy, et al., "Strength Training for Children and Adolescents," *Journal of American Orthopedic Surgery* 9 (2001): 29–36.

2. Goeken, et al., "Sport Stretching: Effect on Passive Muscle Stiffness of Short Hamstrings," *Archives of Physical Medicine and Rehabilitation* 77, no. 7 (July 1996): 688–692.

3. Bojsen-Moller, et al., "A Biomechanical Evaluation of Cyclic and Static Stretch in human Skeletal Muscle," *International Journal of Sports Medicine* 19, no. 5 (July 1998): 310–316.

4. Hahn, et al., "Influences of Strength, Stretching, and Circulatory Exercises on Flexibility Parameters of the Human Hamstrings," *International Journal of Sports Medicine* 18, no. 5 (July 1997): 340–346.

5. Kjaer, et al., "A Mechanism for Altered Flexibility in Human Skeletal Muscle," *Journal of Physiology* 497 (December 1996): 857.

6. S.J. Ingraham, "The Role of Flexibility in Injury Prevention and Athletic Performance: Have We Stretched the Truth?" *Minnesota Medicine* 86, no. 5 (May 2003): 58–61.

7. Richard A. Schmidt, *Motor Learning and Performance* (Champaign, Ill.: Human Kinetics, 2004).

Appendix

SUGGESTED NUTRITIONAL HEALTH READINGS

Allan, Christian, Ph.D., and Dr. Wolfgang Lutz. *Life Without Bread.* Los Angeles: Keats Publishing, 2000.

Bowden, Johnny. *Living the Low-Carb Life.* New York: Sterling Publishing, 2005.

Eades, Dr. Michael, and Dr. MaryDan Eades. *The Protein Power Lifeplan.* New York: Warner Books, 2000.

Mercola, Dr. Joseph. *The No Grain Diet.* New York: Dutton Publishing, 2003.

Planck, Nina. *Real Food: What to Eat and Why.* New York: Bloomsbury Publishing, 2006.

SUGGESTED NUTRITIONAL COOKBOOKS

Barnaby, Karen. *The Low-Carb Gourmet: 250 Delicious and Satisfying Recipes.* Emmaus, Penn.: Rodale Books, 2004.

Eades, Dr. Michael, and Dr. MaryDan Eades. *The Low-Carb Comfort Cook Book.* Hoboken, N.J.: John Wiley and Sons, 2003.

_____. *The 30-Day Low-Carb Diet Solution.* Hoboken, N.J.: John Wiley and Sons, 2003.

PARENTING BOOKS

Glasser, Dr. William. *The Choice Theory.* New York: Harper, 1999.

WEB RESOURCES

Grassland Beef

www.grasslandbeef.com
A great resource for choosing grass-fed meats and other healthy food choices.

Hawthorne Valley Farms

www.hawthornevalleyfarm.org
Here you can learn about and purchase raw milk products.

NUTRITIONAL DIET INFORMATION

Protein Power

www.ProteinPower.com
The official website of my friends and authors Dr. Michael and Dr. MaryDan Eades. It's full of valid and helpful nutritional info. A quick glance at their blogs on a daily basis will keep you healthy and wise.

Living LaVida Low Carb

www.livinglavidalowcarb.com
The official website of Jimmy Moore who successfully lost over 200 pounds eating and exercising as this book suggests. He frequently has fantastic interviews with leading health experts.

EQUIPMENT RESOURCES

PDA Design

www.fractionalplates.com/fractional.html
Where you can get small add-on weight plates as small as 1/8 of a pound! You simply place the round plate over the weight stack pin of any machine and you're ready to go.

Sportsmith

www.sportsmith.net/SearchForm.aspx?Search=platemate
Magnetic add-on plates of different shapes and sizes. They come as low as 1 1/4 pounds.

Metronomes

www.metronomeonline.com
This is a fee metronome you can use on your computer

www.metronomes.net
This site has a wide array of metronomes

DUMBBELLS AND OTHER EQUIPMENT

The Gym Source

www.gymsource.com
Almost anything you'd ever need for creating a great home gym.

Bowflex

www.bowflexselecttech.com

Excellent adjustable dumbbell. Increases are in small, 2 1/2-pound increments.

Repetition Counter

www.tallycounterstore.com

SCIENTIFIC SUPPORT FOR *STRONG KIDS, HEALTHY KIDS*

Pediatric Exercise Science, **2005**: "Early Muscular Fitness Adaptations in Children in Response to Two Different Resistance Training Regimens"

Researchers found that both high repetitions (15 to 20) and lower repetition ranges (6 to 10) produced similar but statistically significant outcomes in strength.

American Heart Association (2000).

The AHA evaluated and approved research indicating that strength training improves all of the health risk factors that are checked by a physician at a physical exam (e.g., cholesterol, blood pressure, body fat, insulin sensitivity, and bone density).

Avery Faigenbaum et al. (1993, 1995, 1996, 1999).

In numerous studies, Avery Faigenbaum and colleagues have shown that children who strength train once or twice a week for 20 to 30 minutes gain significant muscle strength and endurance, positively change their body composition, and improve athletic performance.

Ades, Blair et al. (2002).

Strength training improves treadmill-walking endurance significantly. This is because muscles are the engines of our body. The stronger they become, the better able they are to do anything involving physical work be it treadmill walking or climbing stairs, or running to catch a bus.

Westcott, Tolken, and Wessner (1995).

Fifth-grade students showed significant improvements in body composition from 50-minute sessions including 7 strength-training exercises twice a week for 8 weeks. Results were a 2.7 percent reduction in fat, a 3-pound decrease in fat weight, and a 2.5-pound increase in muscle weight.

Amirfalah and Baum (1995).

Strength training improves cardiovascular efficiency and blood lipid profiles.

Cohen (1995).

A three-year study showed no improvement in body composition of middle-school students from standard physical fitness programs.

Ignacio and Mahon (1995).

Fifth-grade students who took hour-long aerobic exercise classes three times a week for ten weeks showed no change in body composition.

Campbell et al. (1996).

Strength training stimulates metabolic activity and increases basal metabolic rate.

Westcott, Long, and La Rosa Loud (2003)

An eight-week study of seventh graders who experienced significant improvements in body composition from three weekly 40-minute activity sessions that included six strength exercises. Students lost 2.8 percent fat, 5 total pounds of fat, and gained 4.3 pounds of lean weight.

Halbertsma, J.P., and L.N. Goeken. "Stretching Exercises: Effect on Passive Extensibility and Stiffness in Short Hamstrings of Healthy Subjects." *International Journal of Sports Medicine 18, no. 5* (July 1997): 340–346.

Department of Rehabilitation Medicine, University of Groningen, Archives of *Physical Medicine and Rehabilitation* 76, no. 6 (June 1995): 587.

Conclusion: "It is concluded that stretching exercises do not make short hamstrings any longer or less stiff, but only influence the stretch tolerance."

Wiemann, K., and K. Hahn, "Influences of Strength, Stretching and Circulatory Exercises on Flexibility Parameters of the Human Hamstrings." *International Journal of Sports Medicine* 18 no. 5 (July 1997): 340–346.

Conclusion: "The constancy of the muscle resting tension suggests that merely the subjects' tolerance to higher stretching strain brings about the enlargement of ROM after short-term stretching exercises."

Magnusson, S.P., E.B. Simonsen, P. Aagaard, H. Sorensen, and M. Kjaer. "A Mechanism for Altered Flexibility in Human Skeletal Muscle." *Journal of Physiology* (November 1996): 291–298.

Conclusion: "It is concluded that reflex EMG activity does not limit the range of movement during slow stretches and that the increased range of motion achieved from training is a consequence of increased stretch tolerance on the part of the subject rather than a change in the mechanical or viscoelastic properties of the muscle."

Ingraham, S.J., "The Role of Flexibility in Injury Prevention and Athletic Performance: Have We Stretched the Truth?" *Minnesota Medicine* 86, no. 5 (May 2003): 58–61.

Conclusion: "Overall, the evidence suggests that increasing range of motion beyond function through stretching is not beneficial and can actually cause injury and decrease performance. These findings should be used to challenge common warm-up practices in athletics."

THE STRONG KIDS, HEALTHY KIDS
Workout Progress Chart

Name of Exercise	Machine Settings	Date: _____ Body Weight: _____ Daily Notes:		Date: _____ Body Weight: _____ Daily Notes:		Date: _____ Body Weight: _____ Daily Notes:	
		Wgt./Order	Reps	Wgt./Order	Reps	Wgt./Order	Reps

Index